The Pork
Book

Jean Paré

companyscoming.com
visit our ↑ website

Front Cover Crown Pork Roast, page 104

Props Courtesy Of:
Canhome Global
Chintz & Company
Dansk Gifts
The Bay

Back Cover

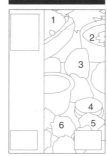

1. Fancy Curried Pork Salad, page 48
2. Jazzy Jerk Soup, page 30
3. Pork Turnovers, page 20
4. Ham Pinwheels, page 16
5. Tandoori Pork Bites, page 19
6. Crunchy Pork Balls, page 21

Props Courtesy Of:
Casa Bugatti
Cherison Enterprises Inc.
Island Pottery Inc.
Pier 1 Imports

Our special thanks to Alberta Pork for their donation of product and nutrition analysis for this book as well as their ongoing support and assistance. For further information, visit www.albertapork.com.

We gratefully acknowledge the following suppliers for their generous support of our Test Kitchen and Photo Studio:

Broil King Barbecues
Corelle ®
Hamilton Beach ® Canada

Lagostina ®
Proctor Silex ® Canada
Tupperware ®

The Pork Book
Copyright © Company's Coming Publishing Limited

Third Printing December 2003

National Library of Canada Cataloguing in Publication

Paré, Jean
      The pork book / Jean Paré.

      (Original series)
Includes index.
ISBN 1-895455-93-6

      1. Cookery (Pork). I. Title. II. Series.

TX749.5.P67P37 2003   641.6'64   C2003-902092-4

Published by
COMPANY'S COMING PUBLISHING LIMITED
2311 – 96 Street
Edmonton, Alberta, Canada T6N 1G3
Tel: (780) 450-6223   Fax: (780) 450-1857
www.companyscoming.com

Visit us on-line

companyscoming.com

Who We Are | **Browse Cookbooks** | **Cooking Tonight?** | **Home**

everyday ingredients

feature recipes

feature recipes — Cooking tonight? Check out this month's **feature recipes**—absolutely FREE!

tips and tricks — Looking for some great kitchen helpers? **tips and tricks** are here to save the day!

reader circle — In search of answers to cooking or household questions? Do you have answers you'd like to share? Join the fun with **reader circle**, our on-line question and answer bulletin board. Great for swapping recipes too!

cooking links — Other interesting and informative web-sites are just a click away with **cooking links**.

cookbook search — Find cookbooks by title, description or food category using **cookbook search**.

contact us — We want to hear from you—**contact us** lets you offer suggestions for upcoming titles, or share your favourite recipes.

Company's Coming

COOKBOOKS®

Canada's
**most popular
cookbooks!**

Company's Coming Cookbook Series

Original Series

- Softcover, 160 pages
- 6" x 9" (15 cm x 23 cm) format
- Lay-flat binding
- Full colour photos
- Nutrition information

Quick & easy recipes, everyday ingredients!

Greatest Hits Series

- Softcover, 106 & 124 pages
- 8" x 9 9/16" (20 cm x 24 cm) format
- Paperback binding
- Full colour photos
- Nutrition information

Lifestyle Series

- Softcover, 160 pages
- 8" x 10" (20 cm x 25 cm) format
- Paperback & spiral binding
- Full colour photos
- Nutrition information

Most Loved Series

- Hardcover, 128 pages
- 8 3/4" x 8 3/4" (22 cm x 22 cm) format
- Full colour throughout
- Nutrition information

Special Occasion Series

- Hardcover & softcover, 192 pages
- 8 1/2" x 11" (22 cm x 28 cm) format
- Durable sewn binding
- Full colour throughout
- Nutrition information

See page 157 for a complete listing of **all** cookbooks or visit companyscoming.com

Table of Contents

D1114110

The Company's Coming Story

Jean Paré grew up understanding that the combination of family, friends and home cooking is the essence of a good life. From her mother she learned to appreciate good cooking, while her father praised even her earliest attempts. When she left home she took with her many acquired family recipes, a love of cooking and an intriguing desire to read recipe books like novels!

"never share a recipe you wouldn't use yourself"

In 1963, when her four children had all reached school age, Jean volunteered to cater the 50th anniversary of the Vermilion School of Agriculture, now Lakeland College. Working out of her home, Jean prepared a dinner for over 1000 people which launched a flourishing catering operation that continued for over eighteen years. During that time she was provided with countless opportunities to test new ideas with immediate feedback—resulting in empty plates and contented customers! Whether preparing cocktail sandwiches for a house party or serving a hot meal for 1500 people, Jean Paré earned a reputation for good food, courteous service and reasonable prices.

"Why don't you write a cookbook?" Time and again, as requests for her recipes mounted, Jean was asked that question. Jean's response was to team up with her son, Grant Lovig, in the fall of 1980 to form Company's Coming Publishing Limited. April 14, 1981 marked the debut of "150 DELICIOUS SQUARES", the first Company's Coming cookbook in what soon would become Canada's most popular cookbook series.

Jean Paré's operation has grown steadily from the early days of working out of a spare bedroom in her home. Full-time staff includes marketing personnel located in major cities across Canada. Home Office is based in Edmonton, Alberta in a modern building constructed specially for the company.

Today the company distributes throughout Canada and the United States in addition to numerous overseas markets, all under the guidance of Jean's daughter, Gail Lovig. Best-sellers many times over in English, Company's Coming cookbooks have also been published in French and Spanish. Familiar and trusted in home kitchens around the world, Company's Coming cookbooks are offered in a variety of formats, including the original softcover series.

Jean Paré's approach to cooking has always called for quick and easy recipes using everyday ingredients. Even when travelling, she is constantly on the lookout for new ideas to share with her readers. At home, she can usually be found researching and writing recipes, or working in the company's test kitchen. Jean continues to gain new supporters by adhering to what she calls "the golden rule of cooking": never share a recipe you wouldn't use yourself. It's an approach that works— *millions of times over!*

Foreword

Today's pork is low in fat, delicious and versatile. The many ways to serve this lean, nutritious meat are only limited by your imagination! *The Pork Book* contains tasty recipes that will inspire your creative side and stimulate your appetite.

In recent years, pork has grown in popularity—and for good reason! It's a healthy alternative to other meats and it tastes great. For example, lean pork tenderloin has the same amount of fat per serving as skinless, boneless chicken breast! In addition to being low in fat, pork also provides us with a variety of important vitamins and minerals that contribute to a healthy, well-balanced diet. For more information on pork's nutritional benefits, check out Pork Perfection! on page 8.

Today's pork is leaner than ever! In fact, pork is 47% leaner than it was in 1987, and all trimmed cuts today, except ribs, qualify as "lean" or "extra lean." Constant improvements in feeding, breeding and trimming practices have resulted in a leaner, safer, more nutritious product. Because today's pork is so lean, it tends to become dry and flavourless when it's overcooked. The secret to achieving tender, juicy results every time is to cook pork to an internal temperature of 160°F (70°C). Or if you're like me and you prefer more general estimates, plan on cooking your pork for approximately 20 to 25 minutes per pound (45 to 55 minutes per kilogram) until the internal juices run clear.

We want you to be able to prepare pork with creativity and confidence. For more information on the different retail cuts of pork, serving sizes, cooking methods and safety tips, see pages 9 through 11.

One of the best things about pork is its versatility. It lends itself to many different

presentations, from a simple ham sandwich to an elegant crown roast. Serve pork as a main dish or as an ingredient in casseroles, stews, stir-fries, soups and salads. Jazz it up with sweet and savoury accompaniments, such as applesauce, spiced plums, fresh fruit, tangy mustards or grilled pineapple. The possibilities are endless!

Explore the wide range of delicious dishes featured in *The Pork Book*. Have fun making traditional favourites and enjoy experimenting with new tastes. Your family and friends will marvel at the results!

Jean Paré

Each recipe has been analyzed using the most up-to-date version of the Canadian Nutrient File from Health Canada, which is based on the United States Department of Agriculture (USDA) Nutrient Database. If more than one ingredient is listed (such as "hard margarine or butter"), then the first ingredient is used in the analysis. Where an ingredient reads "sprinkle," "optional," or "for garnish," it is not included as part of the nutrition information.

Andrea (Smith) Licursi, M.Sc., R.D.
Health and Nutrition Specialist
Alberta Pork

Pork Perfection!

Today's pork is leaner than ever and it's packed with nutrition! For starters, pork is the best dietary source of thiamin (vitamin B1). This vitamin supports healthy nerve functioning, energy production, growth, and digestive and neurological health. Pork is also a good source of riboflavin (B2), niacin (B3), vitamins B6 and B12, zinc, phosphorus, magnesium and iron.

In addition, an average cooked serving of pork (3 oz., 85 g) is a complete source of protein, providing us with all nine essential amino acids that cannot be made by the body. Protein is vital to a healthy diet as it helps to keep our immune system strong and to build, repair and maintain body tissues.

Canada's Food Guide to Healthy Eating recommends that we eat 2 to 3 servings of meat or meat alternatives daily and choose leaner meats more often. Surprisingly, many people, especially women, are still not meeting the minimum requirement of 2 servings per day. Don't deprive yourself any longer!

Lean meats, such as pork, can be part of a low-fat, low-cholesterol lifestyle. Unlike other types of meat, lean pork is very easy to identify. Most of the fat content shows up as a visible band around the outer edge or through the middle (in a roast). Therefore, if the pork looks lean, it probably is. In fact, all trimmed cuts of pork (except for ribs) are considered "lean" or "extra lean," according to Health Canada's nutrition labelling guidelines. That means they contain less than 10% fat!

Cut Out The Fat! Keep In The Protein!

A 3 1/2 oz. (100 g) portion of raw, **untrimmed** pork contains: 192 calories, 21 g of protein, 10 g of fat and 0 g of carbohydrate.
A 3 1/2 oz. (100 g) portion of raw, **trimmed** pork contains: 139 calories, 22 g of protein, 5 g of fat and 0 g of carbohydrate.

Retail Cuts

A side of pork is composed of four main sections—loin, shoulder, leg and belly. When purchasing pork, keep in mind that cuts from the different sections will have different characteristics and different values. Some cuts will suit a particular recipe while other cuts will not.

SECTION	SUB-SECTION	RETAIL CUTS	DESCRIPTION
LOIN	rib end (closest to shoulder) tenderloin (sirloin) end loin centre-cut tenderloin	rib end, centre-cut and tenderloin end roasts/steaks; crown roasts; butterflied steaks; chops; rib end country-style ribs; back ribs; etc.	tender and lean most expensive cuts ideally cooked using dry heat methods
SHOULDER	shoulder picnic shoulder butt (blade)	butt, picnic and capicolla roasts/ steaks; chops; riblets; cutlets; cubes; strips; etc.	butt is most popular capicolla is boneless section of butt internal marbling visible picnic often cured like ham
LEG	outside inside tip	outside, inside, tip roasts/steaks; centre-cut, shank roasts; butt roasts; cutlets; strips; cubes; hock; etc.	leg is as lean as loin and can be as tender inside sub-section is most tender
BELLY	ribs side pork	spareribs; St. Louis-style ribs; sweet & sour cut ribs; rib fingers; sliced side of pork; etc.	contains more fat ribs are great barbecued/grilled

What Is A Serving Size?

An easy guideline to remember...

One serving (3 oz., 85 g) of lean, trimmed, cooked meat is about the size of a deck of playing cards.

Cooking Methods

There are two main methods of cooking pork—dry heat and moist heat. The method you choose will depend on the cut of pork and your personal preference. Moist heat is often better for tougher cuts, as it will help tenderize them during the cooking process.

Dry Heat Methods

Barbecuing (Grilling): Best for side and back ribs, roasts, ground pork burgers, chops, steaks, sausages and kabobs.

Broiling: Best for kabobs, side and back ribs, chops, steaks and ground pork burgers.

Frying: Best for chops, steaks, ground pork burgers, sausage, pork cubes, tenderloin and leg cutlets.

Roasting: Best for loin, leg, crown and shoulder roasts. Cooking times will vary depending on thickness and length of roast and whether cut is boneless or bone-in, but plan on cooking for 20 to 25 minutes per pound (45 to 55 minutes per kilogram).

Stir-frying: Best for pork strips, pork cubes and ground pork.

Moist Heat Methods

Braising: Best for shoulder picnic roasts, leg steaks/roasts, loin and rib steaks/chops, shoulder steaks/chops, leg and loin cutlets, ribs, pork cubes, pork strips and leg tip roasts. Braising tenderizes tougher cuts.

Stewing: Best for pork cubes, pork strips, ribs and shoulder chops/steaks. Uses more liquid and smaller pieces of meat than braising.

Cooking Yields

Do you ever have trouble deciding how much meat to buy for your meal? Because water evaporates during the cooking process, allow about 4 oz. (113 g) of raw pork for every 3 1/2 oz. (100 g) cooked serving. Refer to this chart for more information.

COOKED SERVINGS	Servings/lb.	Servings/kg
Side or Back Ribs	1–2	3–5
Bone–In Roasts	2–3	5–6
Butt Steak	2–3	5–6
Steaks, Cutlets, Chops	3–4	7–8
Boneless Roasts	3–4	7–8
Ground Pork Sausage	3–4	7–8

Be Safe, Be Healthy

1. Never let raw and cooked foods come into contact with same surfaces or with each other.

2. Always wash hands with warm, soapy water before and after handling raw meat.

3. Sanitize cutting boards often. Soak in bleach and water solution using 1 tsp. (5 mL) bleach for every 3 cups (750 mL) water.

4. Use clean utensils for each food item.

5. Never leave perishable foods at room temperature for more than 2 hours.

6. Always defrost meat in refrigerator or microwave. If you defrost meat in microwave, cook immediately.

7. Store leftovers in refrigerator within 1 hour of when they were served.

8. Marinate meats in refrigerator.

9. Use a meat thermometer to determine doneness of roasts—don't guess! Insert thermometer into thickest part of roast. When testing stuffed roasts, keep tip of thermometer in roast, not stuffing. Cook to internal temperature of 160°F (70°C). A small amount of pink may remain in centre but juices should run clear.

10. Never store raw pork at temperatures higher than 40°F (4°C).

11. If you are ever unsure about the safety of a food item, throw it out. If it smells or looks suspicious, don't taste it—toss it!

Pork Industry Positives

Today's pork industry is more productive, more closely monitored and safer than ever before. Canadian Pork Producers want to ensure that domestic and international consumers are secure in the knowledge that they are purchasing a safe and wholesome product. To ensure the consistent production of quality pork, the Canadian Quality Assurance (CQA™) program was developed. This industry-driven program, operated by the Canadian Pork Council (CPC), addresses the issue of food safety, starting with on-farm practices.

Modern housing systems allow farmers to closely monitor their animals' health while protecting the pigs from parasites, infections, insects and predators. The Canadian meat inspection system is second to none, which is why trichinosis (a parasitic disease) is no longer a concern. In fact, there has not been a single reported case of trichinosis attributable to pork in over 25 years.

11

Peanut Pork Balls

*These dark brown pork balls are sweet and nutty. Roll them ahead
of time and chill until 30 minutes prior to cooking.
These are perfect for a cocktail party.*

Chinese dried mushrooms	4	4
Boiling water, to cover		
Lean ground pork	1 lb.	454 g
Garlic cloves, minced (or 1 tsp., 5 mL, powder)	4	4
Fine dry bread crumbs	2/3 cup	150 mL
Cornstarch	1/2 cup	125 mL
Chopped fresh cilantro (or fresh parsley)	2 tbsp.	30 mL
Indonesian sweet (or thick) soy sauce	3 tbsp.	50 mL
Sweet (or regular) chili sauce	3 tbsp.	50 mL
Crunchy peanut butter (see Note)	3 tbsp.	50 mL
Large egg	1	1
Pine nuts, toasted (see Tip, page 105) and chopped	1/3 cup	75 mL
Cooking oil, for deep-frying		
DIPPING SAUCE		
Lime juice	1/4 cup	60 mL
Sweet (or regular) chili sauce	3 tbsp.	50 mL
Soy sauce	2 tsp.	10 mL
Fish sauce	1 tsp.	5 mL

Put mushrooms into small bowl. Add boiling water. Let stand for 20 minutes until softened. Drain. Remove and discard stems. Chop caps finely.

Process next 9 ingredients in food processor until smooth. Transfer to large bowl.

Add mushrooms and pine nuts. Mix well. Shape into balls using 1 tbsp. (15 mL) mixture for each.

Deep-fry, in batches, in hot (350°F, 175°C) cooking oil for 1 to 2 minutes until browned and completely cooked. Remove to paper towels to drain.

(continued on next page)

Dipping Sauce: Combine all 4 ingredients in separate small bowl. Makes about 1/2 cup (125 mL) sauce. Serve with pork balls. Makes about 52 pork balls.

1 pork ball with 1/2 tsp. (2 mL) sauce: 60 Calories; 3.4 g Total Fat (1.6 g Mono, 0.8 g Poly, 0.8 g Sat); 8 mg Cholesterol; 5 g Carbohydrate; trace Fibre; 3 g Protein; 45 mg Sodium

Note: Add finely chopped peanuts to smooth peanut butter if you don't have crunchy on hand.

Ham Skewers

*A fast appetizer to make so that guests can
munch while they wait for dinner.*

Grape jelly	1/2 cup	125 mL
Chili sauce	2 tbsp.	30 mL
Lemon juice	2 tbsp.	30 mL
Sweet hot mustard	1 tsp.	5 mL
Onion salt	1/4 tsp.	1 mL
Ham steak (3/4 inch, 2 cm, thick), cut into 3/4 inch (2 cm) cubes	1 lb.	454 g
Fresh (or canned) pineapple (or melon or firm mango) chunks (optional)	15	15
Bamboo skewers (4 inch, 10 cm, length), soaked in water for 10 minutes	15	15

Mix first 5 ingredients in small saucepan. Heat and stir on medium-low until smooth.

Thread 2 to 3 ham cubes and 1 pineapple chunk alternately onto skewers. Preheat electric grill for 5 minutes or gas barbecue to medium-high. Cook skewers on greased grill, or broil on greased broiler pan on top rack in oven, for about 10 minutes, brushing with jelly mixture and turning often, until bubbling and glazed. Makes 15 skewers.

1 skewer: 83 Calories; 1.7 g Total Fat (0.7 g Mono, 0.2 g Poly, 0.5 g Sat); 16 mg Cholesterol; 12 g Carbohydrate; trace Fibre; 5 g Protein; 377 mg Sodium

Spicy Sausage Rolls

Flaky, golden pastry surrounds a delicious pork filling.
These tasty two-bite appetizers are sure to be a hit!

Lean ground pork (not previously frozen)	1 lb.	454 g
Large egg, fork-beaten	1	1
Seasoned salt	1 tsp.	5 mL
Coarsely ground pepper (or 1/4 tsp., 1 mL, pepper)	1/2 tsp.	2 mL
Cayenne pepper	1/2 tsp.	2 mL
Dried whole oregano	1/4 tsp.	1 mL
Dried thyme	1/4 tsp.	1 mL
Garlic powder (optional)	1/4 tsp.	1 mL
Onion powder	1/4 tsp.	1 mL
Package of frozen puff pastry, thawed according to package directions	14 oz.	397 g
Large egg	1	1
Milk	1 tbsp.	15 mL

TOPPINGS (optional)
Sesame seeds
Poppy seeds
Cumin seed
Paprika

Combine first 9 ingredients in medium bowl. Divide into 4 portions. Shape each into 8 inch (20 cm) long roll. Place on ungreased baking sheet. Freeze, uncovered, for about 1 1/2 hours until firm.

Roll out each pastry half to 1/8 inch (3 mm) thickness (about 10 × 10 inch, 25 × 25 cm, square). Cut each square into 2 rectangles. Place 1 pork roll on long side of each rectangle.

Beat second egg and milk with fork in small dish. Dampen edge of pastry furthest from pork roll with egg mixture. Roll up, jelly roll-style. Press long edge to seal. Brush rolls with egg mixture. Cut into 1 inch (2.5 cm) pieces.

Toppings: Sprinkle with your choice of toppings. Arrange rolls, standing upright, on greased baking sheets. Bake in 400°F (205°C) oven for about 25 minutes until golden. Makes 32 rolls.

1 roll: 104 Calories; 7.2 g Total Fat (3.8 g Mono, 0.8 g Poly, 2.1 g Sat); 19 mg Cholesterol; 6 g Carbohydrate; trace Fibre; 4 g Protein; 71 mg Sodium

Pictured on page 17.

Sweet Cold Pork Slices

These tender pork slices have attractive red edges and a spicy kick. Arrange them on a pretty plate to serve or on toasted baguette slices with a dot of mayonnaise or chutney on top for canapés. Used in Pork Wonton Soup, page 32.

MARINADE

Indonesian sweet (or thick) soy sauce	1/4 cup	60 mL
Fancy (mild) molasses	1/4 cup	60 mL
Apple cider vinegar	1/4 cup	60 mL
Chili paste (sambal oelek)	1 tbsp.	15 mL
Garlic cloves, minced (or 1/2 tsp., 2 mL, powder)	2	2
Red food colouring (optional)	1 tsp.	5 mL
Pork tenderloins (about 1 lb., 454 g, each), trimmed of fat	2	2

Water

Marinade: Combine first 6 ingredients in small bowl. Pour into large resealable freezer bag.

Add pork. Seal. Turn until coated. Marinate in refrigerator overnight or for up to 24 hours, turning several times. Pour marinade into small saucepan. Boil, uncovered, for 5 minutes.

Place pork on greased rack in roasting pan containing about 1/2 inch (12 mm) water. Cook in 275°F (140°C) oven for 2 hours, adding water as necessary to maintain 1/2 inch (12 mm). Turn pork several times, brushing generously with marinade. Cool completely before cutting into 1/4 inch (6 mm) thick slices. Makes about 50 slices.

1 slice: 28 Calories; 0.5 g Total Fat (0.2 g Mono, 0.1 g Poly, 0.2 g Sat); 11 mg Cholesterol; 1 g Carbohydrate; 0 g Fibre; 4 g Protein; 11 mg Sodium

Pictured on page 108.

Paré Pointer
Knock! Knock! Who's there? Doris. Doris who?
Doris locked—that's why I knocked.

Ham Pinwheels

These attractive, tasty pinwheels with a soft, creamy filling can be made ahead. Garnish with fresh chives or green onions for a finished look.

Block of cream cheese, softened	8 oz.	250 g
Worcestershire sauce	1 tbsp.	15 mL
Chopped fresh chives (or finely chopped green onion)	4 tsp.	20 mL
Dry mustard	1/2 tsp.	2 mL
Cooked ham slices (square slices best)	15	15
Melba toast rounds (or English cucumber slices or toasted baguette slices)	50	50

Mash cream cheese, Worcestershire sauce, chives and mustard in small bowl until smooth.

Spread each ham slice with 1 tbsp. (15 mL) cream cheese mixture. Lay 3 slices end to end. Roll up from short side. Wrap tightly in plastic wrap. Repeat to make 5 rolls. Chill for at least 3 hours before serving.

Cut rolls into 1/4 inch (6 mm) thick slices. Lay, cut side down, on melba toast rounds. Makes about 50 appetizers.

1 appetizer: 29 Calories; 1.9 g Total Fat (0.6 g Mono, 0.1 g Poly, 1.1 g Sat); 6 mg Cholesterol; 2 g Carbohydrate; trace Fibre; 1 g Protein; 22 mg Sodium

Pictured on page 18 and on back cover.

1. Spicy Sausage Rolls, page 14
2. Bacon-Wrapped Bananas, page 25
3. Spicy Peanut Sauce, page 23
4. Korean Skewered Pork, page 22
5. Pork And Pear Tartlets, page 26

Props Courtesy Of: Linens 'N Things

Appetizers

Tandoori Pork Bites

The yogurt and chutney dip offers a
cooling accompaniment to these spicy morsels.

Plain yogurt	2/3 cup	150 mL
Tandoori paste	1/2 cup	125 mL
Mango chutney	1/3 cup	75 mL
Pork tenderloin, trimmed of fat and cut into 3/4 inch (2 cm) cubes	1 lb.	454 g
DIP		
Plain yogurt	1/2 cup	125 mL
Mango chutney	1/3 cup	75 mL

Combine yogurt, tandoori paste and chutney in large bowl.

Add pork. Stir until coated. Cover. Marinate in refrigerator for at least 8 hours or overnight, turning several times. Drain and discard marinade. Preheat gas barbecue to medium. Place pork on greased grill. Cook for 5 to 7 minutes, turning occasionally, until tender.

Dip: Combine yogurt and chutney in small bowl. Makes about 1 cup (250 mL) dip. Serve with pork bites. Makes about 32 pork bites.

1 pork bite with 1 1/2 tsp. (7 mL) dip: 33 Calories; 0.7 g Total Fat (0.3 g Mono, 0.1 g Poly, 0.3 g Sat); 10 mg Cholesterol; 2 g Carbohydrate; 0 g Fibre; 4 g Protein; 51 mg Sodium

Pictured on page 18 and on back cover.

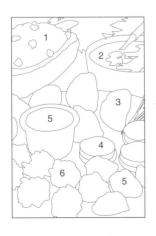

1. Fancy Curried Pork Salad, page 48
2. Jazzy Jerk Soup, page 30
3. Pork Turnovers, page 20
4. Ham Pinwheels, page 16
5. Tandoori Pork Bites, above
6. Crunchy Pork Balls, page 21

Props Courtesy Of: Casa Bugatti
Cherison Enterprises Inc.
Island Pottery Inc.
Pier 1 Imports

Pork Turnovers

These are wonderful little pastries with a sweet, tangy
filling. These can be frozen and reheated for those unexpected guests.

Olive (or cooking) oil	1 tbsp.	15 mL
Finely chopped red pepper	1/2 cup	125 mL
Finely chopped onion	1/2 cup	125 mL
Garlic cloves, minced (or 1/2 tsp., 2 mL, powder)	2	2
Prosciutto (or deli) ham slices, finely chopped	3	3
Lean ground pork	4 oz.	113 g
Roma (plum) tomato, finely chopped	1	1
Chopped fresh sweet basil (or 3/4 tsp., 4 mL, dried)	1 tbsp.	15 mL
Sour cream	1/4 cup	60 mL
Finely grated fresh Parmesan cheese	1/4 cup	60 mL
Package of frozen puff pastry, thawed according to package directions	14 oz.	397 g
Large egg, fork-beaten	1	1
Sesame seeds	3 tbsp.	50 mL

Heat olive oil in large frying pan on medium. Add red pepper, onion and garlic. Cook for 5 to 10 minutes, stirring often, until onion is softened.

Add ham and ground pork. Scramble-fry on medium-high for about 5 minutes until browned. Remove from heat.

Add next 4 ingredients. Mix well.

Roll out each pastry half to 1/8 inch (3 mm) thickness, about 8 x 8 inch (20 x 20 cm) square. Cut circles from pastry using 3 inch (7.5 cm) fluted cookie cutter. Lightly brush edge of circles with egg. Spoon 1 tsp. (5 mL) pork mixture down centre of each. Fold over to enclose filling. Pinch edges together to seal. Brush tops with egg.

Sprinkle with sesame seeds. Place on ungreased baking sheets. Bake in 375°F (190°C) oven for 20 to 25 minutes until golden. Makes about 36 turnovers.

1 turnover: 88 Calories; 6.2 g Total Fat (3.3 g Mono, 0.9 g Poly, 1.7 g Sat); 4 mg Cholesterol; 6 g Carbohydrate; trace Fibre; 3 g Protein; 62 mg Sodium

Pictured on page 18 and on back cover.

Crunchy Pork Balls

These tasty, golden morsels are delicious with a sweet chili sauce or soy sauce.

Day-old white bread slices, crusts removed	12	12
Lean ground pork	1 lb.	454 g
Raw medium shrimp, peeled, deveined and chopped	4 oz.	113 g
Hoisin sauce	2 tbsp.	30 mL
Szechuan seasoning	1/2 tsp.	2 mL
Garlic cloves, minced (or 1/2 tsp., 2 mL, powder)	2	2
Salt	1/2 tsp.	2 mL
Chopped fresh cilantro (or fresh parsley)	2 tbsp.	30 mL

Cooking oil, for deep-frying

Roll out each bread slice to 1/8 inch (3 mm) thickness. Cut into 1/8 inch (3 mm) cubes. Place in shallow dish or on waxed paper.

Process next 7 ingredients in blender until smooth. Shape rounded teaspoonfuls into balls. Press each ball into bread cubes until well coated.

Deep-fry, in batches, in hot (350°F, 175°C) cooking oil for 1 to 2 minutes until golden brown and no longer pink inside. Remove to paper towels to drain. Makes about 54 appetizers.

1 appetizer: 39 Calories; 1.7 g Total Fat (0.7 g Mono, 0.3 g Poly, 0.5 g Sat); 8 mg Cholesterol; 3 g Carbohydrate; trace Fibre; 3 g Protein; 69 mg Sodium

Pictured on page 18 and on back cover.

Paré Pointer
Novices thought they should wear two pairs of pants when golfing in case they got a hole in one.

Dry Baby Back Ribs

These well-seasoned ribs are very tender and meaty.
A classic finger food that is so easy to make!

Baby back pork ribs, cut into 1-bone portions	3 lbs.	1.4 kg
Lemon pepper	1 tbsp.	15 mL
Garlic salt	1 1/2 tsp.	7 mL
Seasoned salt	1 1/2 tsp.	7 mL

Put ribs into large roasting pan. Cover. Bake in 300°F (150°C) oven for 45 minutes. Discard juices.

Combine lemon pepper, garlic salt and seasoned salt in small bowl. Sprinkle about 1 tbsp. (15 mL) over ribs. Stir well. Cover. Bake in 250°F (120°C) oven for 1 hour. Sprinkle with remaining lemon pepper mixture. Stir. Bake, uncovered, for 45 to 50 minutes, stirring once or twice, until golden brown and slightly dry. Makes about 25 ribs.

1 rib: 159 Calories; 13.2 g Total Fat (6 g Mono, 1.1 g Poly, 4.9 g Sat); 45 mg Cholesterol; trace Carbohydrate; trace Fibre; 9 g Protein; 248 mg Sodium

Korean Skewered Pork

These tender, tasty skewers have a mild ginger and sesame
flavour. For thin, even slices, ask your butcher to slice the roast with
a meat cutter. Serve with Spicy Peanut Sauce, page 23.

MARINADE		
Low-sodium soy sauce	1/3 cup	75 mL
Sweet (or regular) chili sauce	1/4 cup	60 mL
Sesame oil	1 tbsp.	15 mL
Sesame seeds, toasted (see Tip, page 105)	1 tbsp.	15 mL
Garlic cloves, minced (or 1 tsp., 5 mL, powder)	4	4
Brown sugar, packed	2 tsp.	10 mL
Finely grated peeled gingerroot	1 tsp.	5 mL
Chili paste (sambal oelek)	1 tsp.	5 mL
Boneless pork shoulder butt roast	1 1/2 lbs.	680 g

(continued on next page)

Bamboo skewers (8 inch, 20 cm, length),   12   12
    soaked in water for 10 minutes

Marinade: Combine first 8 ingredients in small bowl. Pour into large resealable freezer bag.

Cut roast across grain on diagonal into 1/8 inch (3 mm) thick slices. Add to marinade. Seal. Turn until coated. Marinate in refrigerator for 4 to 5 hours, turning once or twice. Drain and discard marinade.

Thread pork loosely, accordion-style, onto skewers. Preheat electric grill for 5 minutes or gas barbecue to medium-high. Cook skewers on greased grill, or broil on greased broiler pan on top rack in oven, for 4 to 5 minutes per side until desired doneness. Makes 12 skewers.

1 skewer: 108 Calories; 5.3 g Total Fat (2.3 g Mono, 1 g Poly, 1.5 g Sat); 36 mg Cholesterol; 2 g Carbohydrate; trace Fibre; 12 g Protein; 193 mg Sodium

Pictured on page 17.

Spicy Peanut Sauce

This thick sauce is mildly spiced with a sweet, yet tangy flavour.
Serve with Korean Skewered Pork, page 22.

Water	1/2 cup	125 mL
Peanut butter	1/2 cup	125 mL
Finely chopped roasted salted peanuts	2 tbsp.	30 mL
Brown sugar, packed	1 tbsp.	15 mL
Soy sauce	2 tsp.	10 mL
Chili paste (sambal oelek)	1/2 tsp.	2 mL
Garlic powder	1/2 tsp.	2 mL
Lime juice	1 tsp.	5 mL

Chopped roasted salted peanuts,
    for garnish
Chopped fresh parsley, for garnish

Combine first 7 ingredients in small saucepan. Heat and stir on medium for 4 to 5 minutes until boiling.

Stir in lime juice. Cool to room temperature.

Garnish with peanuts and parsley. Makes 1 cup (250 mL).

2 tbsp. (30 mL): 122 Calories; 9.7 g Total Fat (4.6 g Mono, 2.8 g Poly, 1.8 g Sat); 0 mg Cholesterol; 6 g Carbohydrate; 1 g Fibre; 5 g Protein; 173 mg Sodium

Pictured on page 17.

Pork Shrimp Rolls

These small rolls are bursting with a delicious pork and shrimp filling.
The rice paper rounds create an attractive look that your guests will love.

Chinese dried mushrooms	6	6
Boiling water, to cover		
Peanut (or cooking) oil	1 tbsp.	15 mL
Garlic cloves, minced (or 1/2 tsp., 2 mL, powder)	2	2
Finely grated peeled gingerroot	2 tsp.	10 mL
Green onions, finely chopped	4	4
Lean ground pork	1 lb.	454 g
Prepared chicken broth	1/4 cup	60 mL
Cornstarch	2 tsp.	10 mL
Hoisin sauce	2 tbsp.	30 mL
Oyster sauce	2 tbsp.	30 mL
Raw medium shrimp, peeled, deveined and finely chopped	4 oz.	113 g
Can of water chestnuts, drained and finely chopped	8 oz.	227 mL
Chopped choy sum (Chinese flowering cabbage) leaves	2 cups	500 mL
Rice paper rounds (9 inch, 22 cm, diameter)	16	16
DIPPING SAUCE		
Sweet (or regular) chili sauce	2 tbsp.	30 mL
Honey mustard	1 1/2 tbsp.	25 mL
Low-sodium soy sauce	1 tbsp.	15 mL
Indonesian sweet (or thick) soy sauce	1 tbsp.	15 mL

Put mushrooms into small bowl. Add boiling water. Let stand for 20 minutes until softened. Drain. Remove and discard stems. Chop caps finely.

Heat peanut oil in wok or large frying pan. Add garlic, ginger and onion. Cook on medium for about 1 minute until fragrant.

Add ground pork. Scramble-fry on medium-high for about 5 minutes until lightly browned and no longer pink.

(continued on next page)

Appetizers

Combine broth and cornstarch in small cup. Add to pork mixture. Stir well.

Add mushrooms and next 5 ingredients. Stir-fry until shrimp is pink and choy sum is wilted. Cool.

Soak rice paper rounds, a few at a time, in hot water in large pie plate for 2 to 3 minutes until softened. Remove to tea towels to drain. Place 1/4 cup (60 mL) pork mixture down centre of each rice paper round. Roll up to enclose, folding in sides.

Dipping Sauce: Combine all 4 ingredients in separate small bowl. Makes about 1/3 cup (75 mL) sauce. Serve with rolls. Makes 16 rolls.

1 roll with 1 tsp. (5 mL) sauce: 190 Calories; 5.6 g Total Fat (2.4 g Mono, 0.9 g Poly, 1.8 g Sat); 25 mg Cholesterol; 25 g Carbohydrate; 1 g Fibre; 9 g Protein; 179 mg Sodium

Bacon-Wrapped Bananas

This unusual, sweet and salty combination is surprisingly good! Children of all ages will enjoy this fun finger food.

Bacon slices	16	16
Grainy (or Dijon) mustard	4 tsp.	20 mL
Pepper, sprinkle		
Large underripe bananas	2	2

Cook bacon in medium frying pan on medium-high for about 4 minutes until almost crisp. Drain.

Spread each bacon slice with about 1/4 tsp. (1 mL) mustard. Sprinkle with pepper.

Slice each banana into 8 chunks. Wrap 1 bacon slice, mustard-side in, around each banana chunk, securing with cocktail pick. Place on rack in broiler pan. Broil on centre rack in oven for 3 to 4 minutes, turning once or twice, until well browned and bacon is crisp. Remove to paper towels to drain. Remove cocktail picks if desired. Serve warm. Makes 16 appetizers.

1 appetizer: 50 Calories; 3.2 g Total Fat (1.5 g Mono, 0.4 g Poly, 1.1 g Sat); 5 mg Cholesterol; 4 g Carbohydrate; trace Fibre; 2 g Protein; 116 mg Sodium

Pictured on page 17.

Pork And Pear Tartlets

These warm, fragrant tartlets have a lingering blue cheese flavour.
They go perfectly with a glass of port or red wine.

Pastry for 2 crust pie, your own or a mix

Cooking oil	1/2 tbsp.	7 mL
Pork tenderloin, trimmed of fat and finely chopped	1/3 lb.	150 g
Salt	1/8 tsp.	0.5 mL
Pepper	1/8 tsp.	0.5 mL
Finely chopped pear	1/3 cup	75 mL
Crumbled blue cheese (about 1 oz., 28 g)	2 1/2 tbsp.	37 mL
Sour cream	1/2 cup	125 mL
Large eggs	2	2
Ground cinnamon	1/4 tsp.	1 mL

Roll out pastry on lightly floured surface to 1/8 inch (3 mm) thickness. Cut out about 24 circles using 3 inch (7.5 cm) fluted cookie cutter. Press circles into ungreased mini-muffin pans. Cover. Chill for 15 minutes.

Heat cooking oil in medium frying pan on medium. Add pork. Cook for 5 to 7 minutes, stirring occasionally, until lightly browned. Add salt and pepper. Stir. Cool.

Divide pork, pear and cheese among pastry shells.

Combine sour cream, eggs and cinnamon in 1 cup (250 mL) liquid measure. Pour about 2 tsp. (10 mL) into each shell. Bake in 375°F (190°C) oven for about 25 minutes until filling is set and crusts are golden. Makes about 24 tartlets.

1 tartlet: 116 Calories; 7.6 g Total Fat (3.2 g Mono, 0.3 g Poly, 2.1 g Sat); 22 mg Cholesterol; 8 g Carbohydrate; 1 g Fibre; 4 g Protein; 124 mg Sodium

Pictured on page 17.

Glazed Pork Ribs

These sweet, tender ribs are coated in a delicious, dark brown glaze.

Plum sauce	1/2 cup	125 mL
Low-sodium soy sauce	1/4 cup	60 mL
Hoisin sauce	3 tbsp.	50 mL
Liquid honey	3 tbsp.	50 mL
Dry sherry	2 tbsp.	30 mL
Sesame oil	2 tsp.	10 mL
Chinese five-spice powder	1/4 tsp.	1 mL
Pork side spareribs, cut into 3 – 4 bone portions	2 lbs.	900 g
Water	2/3 cup	150 mL

Combine first 7 ingredients in large non-metal bowl.

Add ribs. Stir until coated. Cover. Marinate in refrigerator for at least 24 hours, turning several times. Drain and discard marinade.

Place ribs on greased rack on baking sheet with sides. Carefully pour water into baking sheet. Cook in 350°F (175°C) oven for about 1 hour, turning twice and adding water as necessary to prevent drying, until ribs are browned and tender. Cut into 1-bone portions. Serves 6 to 8.

1 serving: 501 Calories; 29.5 g Total Fat (12.5 g Mono, 3.5 g Poly, 10.7 g Sat); 105 mg Cholesterol; 28 g Carbohydrate; 1 g Fibre; 29 g Protein; 729 mg Sodium

 For a decorative look or an elegant presentation, slice vegetables on the diagonal.

Dutch Pea Soup

*This traditional Dutch soup is known as Erwtensoep (pronounced AIR-tun-soop)
in Holland. If you can't locate rookwurst sausage, use the readily available
European wieners as they are an effective substitute.*

Water	12 cups	3 L
Smoked pork shoulder (or ham hock), about 1 1/2 lbs. (680 g)	1	1
Green split peas, rinsed and drained	2 1/4 cups	550 mL
Medium leeks (white and tender green parts only), thinly sliced	3	3
Diced celery (with leaves)	1 1/2 cups	375 mL
Medium potatoes, diced	2	2
Medium carrots, cut into 1/8 inch (3 mm) thick slices	4	4
Rookwurst sausage (or European wieners), diced	10 1/2 oz.	300 g
Salt	1 1/2 tsp.	7 mL
Pepper	1/4 tsp.	1 mL
Dried thyme	1/4 tsp.	1 mL
Ground nutmeg	1/8 tsp.	0.5 mL

Put water and pork shoulder into large pot or Dutch oven. Bring to a boil.
Skim off foam from around edge of pot.

Add next 5 ingredients. Bring to a boil. Reduce heat to medium-low.
Cover. Simmer for 2 hours, stirring more frequently as soup thickens.
Remove pork shoulder and any large pieces of meat. Remove meat from
bone. Cut into bite-size pieces, discarding any fat, bone and sinew. Return
to split pea mixture.

Add remaining 5 ingredients. Simmer, uncovered, for 30 minutes. Makes
about 13 1/2 cups (3.4 L).

*1 cup (250 mL): 220 Calories; 10 g Total Fat (4.5 g Mono, 1.2 g Poly, 3.5 g Sat); 37 mg Cholesterol;
15 g Carbohydrate; 2 g Fibre; 18 g Protein; 1125 mg Sodium*

Pictured on page 35.

Polish Sauerkraut Soup

This mildly flavoured soup contains hearty chunks of ribs, vegetables and beans.

Bacon slices, diced	4	4
Sweet and sour cut pork ribs, trimmed of fat and cut into 1-bone portions	1 1/2 lbs.	680 g
Garlic clove, minced (or 1/4 tsp., 1 mL, powder)	1	1
Seasoned salt	1/2 tsp.	2 mL
Paprika	1/2 tsp.	2 mL
Pepper	1/4 tsp.	1 mL
Water	6 cups	1.5 L
Cans of stewed tomatoes (with juice), 14 oz. (398 mL) each, slightly mashed	2	2
Jar of sauerkraut, rinsed and drained well	17 1/2 oz.	500 mL
Large onion, chopped	1	1
Sliced carrot	1 cup	250 mL
Bay leaf	1	1
Can of small white beans, rinsed and drained	19 oz.	540 mL
Medium potato, diced	1	1

Cook bacon in large pot or Dutch oven on medium-high for about 5 minutes until starting to brown.

Add next 5 ingredients. Heat and stir for about 6 minutes until ribs are browned.

Add next 6 ingredients. Bring to a boil. Reduce heat to medium-low. Cover. Simmer for about 1 hour until ribs are tender. Remove and discard bay leaf.

Add beans and potato. Bring to a boil. Reduce heat to medium. Cover. Simmer for about 30 minutes until potato is tender but still holds its shape. Chill, covered, overnight if desired. Skim off and discard fat from surface before reheating. Makes about 14 cups (3.5 L).

1 cup (250 mL): 170 Calories; 4.9 g Total Fat (2.1 g Mono, 0.6 g Poly, 1.7 g Sat); 35 mg Cholesterol; 17 g Carbohydrate; 5 g Fibre; 15 g Protein; 514 mg Sodium

Jazzy Jerk Soup

Tender pork and diced vegetables add a great deal of substance to this spicy soup. Although it takes a little longer to prepare, the results are worth it! Serve with hot cornbread or ciabatta bread for a hearty dinner.

Cooking oil	2 tbsp.	30 mL
Boneless pork loin, cut into 1/2 inch (12 mm) thick slices	1 lb.	454 g
Finely grated peeled gingerroot	1 tbsp.	15 mL
Paprika	2 tsp.	10 mL
Salt	1 1/2 tsp.	7 mL
Dried crushed chilies	3/4 – 1 tsp.	4 – 5 mL
Dried thyme	1/2 tsp.	2 mL
Ground cinnamon	1/4 tsp.	1 mL
Ground allspice	1/8 tsp.	0.5 mL
Ground cloves	1/16 tsp.	0.5 mL
Coarsely ground pepper	1/16 tsp.	0.5 mL
Chopped onion	1 cup	250 mL
Garlic clove, minced (or 1/4 tsp., 1 mL, powder)	1	1
Prepared chicken broth	4 cups	1 L
Diced potato	2 cups	500 mL
Diced yam (or sweet potato)	2 cups	500 mL
Diced yellow turnip	2 cups	500 mL
Sliced carrot	1 cup	250 mL
Can of stewed tomatoes (with juice), coarsely chopped	14 oz.	398 mL
Can of cream-style corn	14 oz.	398 mL
Fresh spinach, packed, coarsely shredded	2 cups	500 mL

Heat cooking oil in large frying pan on medium-high. Add next 10 ingredients. Cook for about 10 minutes, stirring occasionally, until pork is browned and mixture is very fragrant.

Add onion and garlic. Cook for 2 minutes, stirring and scraping up any brown bits from bottom of pan. (If necessary, 1/4 cup, 60 mL, water may be added to loosen brown bits.) Turn into 3 1/2 to 4 quart (3.5 to 4 L) slow cooker.

Stir in next 7 ingredients. Cover. Cook on Low for 7 to 8 hours or on High for 3 1/2 to 4 hours.

(continued on next page)

Stir in spinach. Cover. Cook on High for about 5 minutes until spinach is wilted. Makes 12 cups (3 L).

1 cup (250 mL): 189 Calories; 4.6 g Total Fat (2.2 g Mono, 1.1 g Poly, 0.8 g Sat); 26 mg Cholesterol; 25 g Carbohydrate; 3 g Fibre; 13 g Protein; 786 mg Sodium

Pictured on page 18 and on back cover.

Spicy Lentil Soup

This red-hot soup will liven up any meal.
It is hearty and inviting with a mild smoky undertone.

Diced bacon (or salt pork)	1/2 cup	125 mL
Sliced chorizo (or hot Italian) sausage	8 oz.	225 g
Chopped onion	1 cup	250 mL
Garlic cloves, minced (or 1/2 tsp., 2 mL, powder)	2	2
Medium carrot, diced	1	1
Celery rib, diced	1	1
Can of roma (plum) tomatoes (with juice), coarsely chopped	28 oz.	796 mL
Can of lentils, rinsed and drained	19 oz.	540 mL
Prepared chicken broth	3 cups	750 mL
Brown sugar, packed	1 tbsp.	15 mL
Diced pickled jalapeño pepper (or other hot pepper)	1 tbsp.	15 mL
Lime juice	2 tsp.	10 mL
Ground cumin	1 tsp.	5 mL
Ground coriander	1/2 tsp.	2 mL
Chopped fresh parsley (or cilantro), for garnish		

Cook bacon in large pot or Dutch oven on medium for about 3 minutes until starting to brown. Add sausage. Heat and stir until browned. Drain and discard all but 2 tsp. (10 mL) drippings from pot.

Add next 4 ingredients. Cook for 2 minutes, stirring and scraping up any brown bits from bottom of pot. (If necessary, 1/4 cup, 60 mL, water may be added to loosen brown bits.)

Add next 8 ingredients. Stir. Bring to a boil. Reduce heat to medium-low. Cover. Simmer for 20 to 30 minutes until carrot is tender.

Sprinkle individual servings with parsley. Makes 9 cups (2.25 L).

1 cup (250 mL): 238 Calories; 11.3 g Total Fat (5 g Mono, 1.5 g Poly, 3.8 g Sat); 27 mg Cholesterol; 22 g Carbohydrate; 3 g Fibre; 14 g Protein; 997 mg Sodium

Pork Wonton Soup

This delicious soup is a meal in a bowl!

Light-coloured soy sauce	1 tbsp.	15 mL
Dry sherry	2 tsp.	10 mL
Cornstarch	2 tsp.	10 mL
Green onion, finely chopped	1	1
Minced garlic (or 1/8 tsp., 0.5 mL, powder), optional	1/2 tsp.	2 mL
Finely grated peeled gingerroot	1/2 tsp.	2 mL
Lean ground pork	6 oz.	170 g
Wonton wrappers	34	34
Water		
Prepared chicken broth	8 cups	2 L
Light-coloured soy sauce	2 tbsp.	30 mL
Sliced carrot	1/2 cup	125 mL
Broccoli florets, cut into smaller florets	6	6
Cauliflower florets, cut into smaller florets	6	6
Fresh snow pea pods, cut if large	6	6
Sweet Cold Pork Slices, page 15 (or other cold pork slices), cut up (optional)	6	6
Fresh medium mushrooms, sliced	3	3
Sliced bok choy (with leaves), packed	2 cups	500 mL
Raw medium shrimp (tails intact), peeled and deveined	6	6
Fresh bean sprouts, for garnish		
Sliced green onion, for garnish		

Combine first 7 ingredients, in order given, in medium bowl.

Lay 1 wrapper on work surface with 1 corner closest to you. Keep unused wrappers covered with damp tea towel to prevent drying out. (1) Place about 1 tsp. (5 mL) pork mixture in centre of wrapper. Dampen finger in small dish of water and draw circle about 1 inch (2.5 cm) from filling. (2) Bring up edges of wrapper and press firmly around filling to seal. Repeat with remaining pork mixture and wrappers, keeping filled wontons covered with damp tea towel. Bring water to a boil in large saucepan. Reduce heat to medium. Cook wontons, in batches, uncovered, for 2 minutes. Drain. Rinse with cold water to cool and to prevent sticking together.

(continued on next page)

Soups

Measure broth and second amount of soy sauce into large pot or Dutch oven. Bring to a boil. Add carrot. Boil, uncovered, for 3 minutes.

Add broccoli and cauliflower. Boil, uncovered, for 1 minute.

Add next 4 ingredients. Cook, uncovered, for 2 minutes.

Add wontons and shrimp. Bring to a boil. Reduce heat to medium-low. Simmer, uncovered, for about 1 minute until shrimp are pink and curled.

Sprinkle individual servings with bean sprouts and onion. Makes 13 cups (3.25 L).

1 cup (250 mL): 360 Calories; 6.3 g Total Fat (2.2 g Mono, 1.2 g Poly, 1.8 g Sat); 24 mg Cholesterol; 56 g Carbohydrate; 4 g Fibre; 20 g Protein; 1328 mg Sodium

Pictured on page 108.

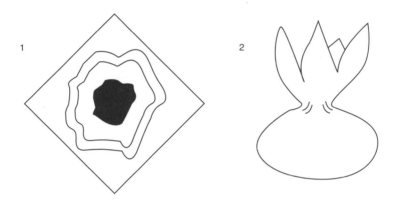

Paré Pointer

A ghost can't keep his trousers up. They have no visible means of support.

Hot And Sour Soup

This soup has a nice range of flavours from hot to sour to sweet.
The fresh, healthy ingredients are colourful and delicious.

Sesame oil	2 tsp.	10 mL
Boneless pork loin roast, cut julienne	8 oz.	225 g
Prepared chicken broth	4 cups	1 L
Can of water chestnuts, drained and chopped	8 oz.	227 mL
Sliced mushrooms	1 cup	250 mL
Thinly sliced celery	1/3 cup	75 mL
Slivered red pepper	1/3 cup	75 mL
Sweet (or regular) chili sauce	1/4 cup	60 mL
Apple cider vinegar	1/4 cup	60 mL
Granulated sugar	1 tbsp.	15 mL
Soy sauce	1 tbsp.	15 mL
Coarsely shredded fresh spinach, lightly packed	1 1/2 cups	375 mL
Fresh bean sprouts, for garnish	1/2 cup	125 mL

Heat sesame oil in large pot or Dutch oven on medium-high. Add pork. Cook for about 5 minutes until lightly browned.

Add next 9 ingredients. Stir. Bring to a boil. Reduce heat to medium-low. Cover. Simmer for 20 minutes to blend flavours.

Stir in spinach. Cover. Simmer for 5 minutes.

Sprinkle individual servings with bean sprouts. Makes 6 1/2 cups (1.6 L).

1 cup (250 mL): 119 Calories; 3.8 g Total Fat (1.5 g Mono, 1 g Poly, 0.9 g Sat); 24 mg Cholesterol; 9 g Carbohydrate; 2 g Fibre; 12 g Protein; 713 mg Sodium

1. Creamy Borscht, page 38
2. Dutch Pea Soup, page 28
3. Ham Hock And Vegetable Soup, page 39

Props Courtesy Of: Canhome Global
The Bay

Quick Leftover Pork Soup

This is a great way to use up leftover pork.
Toss it into this hearty soup for a warm, filling meal.

Cooking oil	2 tsp.	10 mL
Chopped onion	1 1/2 cups	375 mL
Dry white (or alcohol-free) wine (optional)	1/4 cup	60 mL
Water	4 cups	1 L
Can of navy beans (with liquid)	19 oz.	540 mL
Can of Italian-style diced tomatoes (with juice)	14 oz.	398 mL
Diced leftover roast pork	2 cups	500 mL
Diced potato	2 cups	500 mL
Grated carrot	1/2 cup	125 mL
Vegetable bouillon powder	2 tbsp.	30 mL
Pepper	1/2 tsp.	2 mL
Chopped fresh sweet basil (or 1 1/2 tsp., 7 mL, dried)	2 tbsp.	30 mL

Heat cooking oil in large pot or Dutch oven on medium. Add onion. Cook for 5 to 10 minutes, stirring often, until softened.

Add wine. Bring to a boil. Boil for 1 minute.

Add next 8 ingredients. Stir. Bring to a boil. Reduce heat to medium-low. Cover. Simmer for about 45 minutes until potato is soft.

Stir in basil. Makes 9 cups (2.25 L).

1 cup (250 mL): 213 Calories; 3.9 g Total Fat (1.7 g Mono, 0.8 g Poly, 1 g Sat); 26 mg Cholesterol; 28 g Carbohydrate; 2 g Fibre; 17 g Protein; 456 mg Sodium

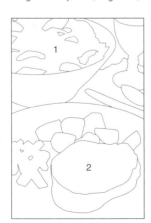

1. Fennel And Sausage Salad, page 43
2. Parmesan-Crumbed Chops, page 70

Creamy Borscht

Pronounced BOHR-sht, this bright pink, creamy soup has a refreshing sweet beet flavour. Serve with a hearty rye bread and garnish with a dollop of sour cream.

Olive (or cooking) oil	2 tsp.	10 mL
Lean ground pork	8 oz.	225 g
Chopped onion	1 cup	250 mL
Garlic clove, minced (or 1/4 tsp., 1 mL, powder), optional	1	1
Sliced mushrooms	2 cups	500 mL
Water	6 cups	1.5 L
Medium beets, peeled and diced (about 1 lb., 454 g)	3	3
Can of navy beans, rinsed and drained	19 oz.	540 mL
Beet leaves (or spinach), lightly packed, shredded	1 cup	250 mL
Diced carrot	1/2 cup	125 mL
Chopped fresh dill (or 1 tbsp., 15 mL, dill weed)	1/4 cup	60 mL
Lemon juice	2 tbsp.	30 mL
Salt	2 tsp.	10 mL
Pepper	1/4 tsp.	1 mL
Water	1/2 cup	125 mL
All-purpose flour	3 tbsp.	50 mL
Homogenized milk (or half-and-half cream)	1 cup	250 mL

Sour cream, for garnish
Chopped fresh dill, for garnish

Heat olive oil in large pot or Dutch oven on medium. Add ground pork, onion and garlic. Cook for 8 to 10 minutes, stirring often, until pork is browned.

Add mushrooms. Cook, stirring occasionally, until liquid is evaporated.

Add next 9 ingredients. Bring to a boil. Reduce heat to medium. Cover. Cook for about 40 minutes until beets are tender.

Stir second amount of water into flour in small cup until smooth. Stir into beet mixture until boiling and slightly thickened. Remove from heat.

Stir in milk.

(continued on next page)

Top individual servings with dollop of sour cream. Sprinkle with dill. Makes about 9 cups (2.25 L).

1 cup (250 mL): 237 Calories; 8.2 g Total Fat (3.3 g Mono, 0.8 g Poly, 3.4 g Sat); 21 mg Cholesterol; 29 g Carbohydrate; 3 g Fibre; 13 g Protein; 914 mg Sodium

Pictured on page 35.

Ham Hock And Vegetable Soup

This comforting soup has a rich, smoky flavour.
Serve with warm crusty bread rolls.

Cooking oil	2 tbsp.	30 mL
Finely chopped onion	1 1/2 cups	375 mL
Finely chopped carrot	1 cup	250 mL
Finely chopped yellow turnip	1 cup	250 mL
Finely chopped celery	1/2 cup	125 mL
Garlic cloves, minced (or 1 tsp., 5 mL, powder)	4	4
Prepared chicken broth	8 cups	2 L
Smoked ham hocks	2 1/4 lbs.	1 kg
Can of diced tomatoes (with juice)	28 oz.	796 mL
Yellow split peas, rinsed and drained	3/4 cup	175 mL
Dry red (or alcohol-free) wine	1/3 cup	75 mL
Tomato paste	1/4 cup	60 mL
Bay leaves	2	2
Diced ham, for garnish		
Chopped fresh parsley, for garnish		

Heat cooking oil in large pot or Dutch oven on medium. Add next 5 ingredients. Stir. Cook for about 10 minutes, stirring often, until onion is softened.

Add next 7 ingredients. Stir. Bring to a boil. Reduce heat to medium-low. Cover. Simmer for 2 hours. Cool. Remove meat from bones. Discard bones. Chop meat. Return to soup. Cover. Chill overnight. Skim off and discard fat from surface. Cook on medium for 10 to 15 minutes, stirring occasionally, until hot. Remove and discard bay leaves.

Garnish individual servings with diced ham and parsley. Makes about 12 1/2 cups (3.1 L).

1 cup (250 mL): 304 Calories; 17.1 g Total Fat (8.1 g Mono, 2.5 g Poly, 5.1 g Sat); 77 mg Cholesterol; 18 g Carbohydrate; 2 g Fibre; 19 g Protein; 1498 mg Sodium

Pictured on page 35.

Main Course Goulash Soup

This deep red soup contains generous chunks of vegetables and small meaty ribs. Provide a "bone bowl" for discarding the rib bones. This big batch of soup may be frozen and reheated, or halved for smaller groups.

Cooking oil	1 tbsp.	15 mL
Sweet and sour cut pork ribs, trimmed of fat and cut into 1-bone portions	2 lbs.	900 g
Paprika	1 tbsp.	15 mL
Salt	2 tsp.	10 mL
Pepper	1 tsp.	5 mL
Medium onion, chopped	1	1
Diced celery	1/2 cup	125 mL
Diced green pepper	1/2 cup	125 mL
Garlic clove, minced (or 1/4 tsp., 1 mL, powder), optional	1	1
Water	8 cups	2 L
Can of diced tomatoes (with juice)	28 oz.	796 mL
Can of tomato paste	5 1/2 oz.	156 mL
Vegetable (or chicken) bouillon powder	2 tbsp.	30 mL
Granulated sugar	1 tsp.	5 mL
Coarsely shredded cabbage	7 cups	1.75 L
Diced potato	2 cups	500 mL
Sliced carrot	1 cup	250 mL
Chopped fresh parsley (or 1 tbsp., 15 mL, flakes)	1/4 cup	60 mL
Chopped fresh dill (or 1 1/2 tsp., 7 mL, dill weed)	2 tbsp.	30 mL
Fresh red chili pepper, finely diced (see Note), or 1/2 – 1 tsp. (2 – 5 mL) dried crushed chilies	1	1

Sour cream, for garnish

Heat cooking oil in large 6 quart (6 L) stockpot on medium. Add ribs, paprika, salt and pepper. Heat and stir for about 5 minutes until ribs are browned.

(continued on next page)

Add next 4 ingredients. Cook for about 5 minutes, stirring often, until vegetables are softened.

Add water, tomatoes, tomato paste, bouillon powder and sugar. Bring to a boil.

Add next 6 ingredients. Stir. Bring to a boil. Reduce heat to medium-low. Cover. Simmer for about 1 1/4 hours, stirring occasionally, until ribs are tender. Chill, covered, overnight if desired. Skim off and discard fat from surface before reheating.

Top individual servings with dollop of sour cream. Makes 20 cups (5 L).

1 cup (250 mL): 126 Calories; 4.7 g Total Fat (2.1 g Mono, 0.7 g Poly, 1.4 g Sat); 29 mg Cholesterol; 11 g Carbohydrate; 2 g Fibre; 11 g Protein; 395 mg Sodium

Note: Wear gloves when chopping chili peppers and avoid touching your eyes.

Ham Slaw

A mild cabbage salad that makes an excellent filling for pita breads or flour tortilla wraps. The addition of ham and cheese enhances the flavour and colour of this dish.

Shredded cabbage	3 cups	750 mL
Diced ham	1 cup	250 mL
Diced Cheddar (or Swiss) cheese	1/2 cup	125 mL
Salad dressing (or mayonnaise)	1/4 cup	60 mL
Granulated sugar	1/2 tsp.	2 mL
Lemon juice	1 tsp.	5 mL

Toss cabbage, ham and cheese in medium bowl.

Combine salad dressing, sugar and lemon juice in small bowl. Let stand for about 5 minutes until sugar is dissolved. Add to cabbage mixture. Toss until coated. Makes 3 cups (750 mL).

3/4 cup (175 mL): 480 Calories; 27.5 g Total Fat (11.1 g Mono, 5.2 g Poly, 9.4 g Sat); 79 mg Cholesterol; 36 g Carbohydrate; 11 g Fibre; 29 g Protein; 1154 mg Sodium

Pictured on page 90.

Sweet Cabbage Salad

*The texture of this salad is very enjoyable. The Asian flavour of
the dressing complements the slight sweetness of the pork slices. So good!*

Hoisin sauce	3 tbsp.	50 mL
Dry sherry (or Chinese cooking wine)	3 tbsp.	50 mL
Sweet (or regular) chili sauce	3 tbsp.	50 mL
Pork tenderloin, trimmed of fat	3/4 lb.	340 g
Finely shredded suey choy (Chinese cabbage)	7 cups	1.75 L
Salted peanuts, toasted (see Tip, page 105)	1/2 cup	125 mL
Coarsely grated carrot	1 1/2 cups	375 mL
Sugar snap peas, trimmed	1 cup	250 mL
Can of water chestnuts, drained and coarsely chopped	8 oz.	227 mL
PEANUT DRESSING		
Peanut oil	1/3 cup	75 mL
White wine vinegar	1/4 cup	60 mL
Low-sodium soy sauce	2 tbsp.	30 mL
Liquid honey	2 tbsp.	30 mL
Sesame oil (optional)	1 tsp.	5 mL

Combine hoisin sauce, sherry and chili sauce in medium bowl.

Add tenderloin. Turn until coated. Cover. Marinate in refrigerator for at
least 8 hours or overnight. Drain and discard marinade. Preheat gas
barbecue to low. Place tenderloin on greased grill. Cook for about 30 minutes,
turning occasionally, until meat thermometer inserted into thickest part
reads 155°F (68°C) or until desired doneness. Cover with foil. Let stand for
10 minutes. Internal temperature should rise to at least 160°F (70°C). Cut
into 1/4 inch (6 mm) thick slices. Transfer to large bowl.

Add next 5 ingredients. Toss.

Peanut Dressing: Combine all 5 ingredients in jar with tight-fitting lid.
Shake well. Makes 1 cup (250 mL) dressing. Drizzle over suey choy
mixture. Toss until coated. Makes about 10 cups (2.5 L).

*1 cup (250 mL): 237 Calories; 12.3 g Total Fat (6.1 g Mono, 3.4 g Poly, 2.1 g Sat);
20 mg Cholesterol; 20 g Carbohydrate; 3 g Fibre; 12 g Protein; 253 mg Sodium*

Pictured on page 72.

Fennel And Sausage Salad

The dramatic colours of this salad are unique and visually striking.
Its lively citrus flavour will awaken your taste buds.

ORANGE DRESSING

Olive (or cooking) oil	1/2 cup	125 mL
Red wine vinegar	1/4 cup	60 mL
Orange juice	1/4 cup	60 mL
Garlic clove, minced (or 1/4 tsp., 1 mL, powder)	1	1
Salt	1/4 tsp.	1 mL
Pepper, just a pinch		
Raisins	1/2 cup	125 mL
Thick pork sausages (about 12 oz., 340 g)	4	4
Medium oranges, peeled and separated into segments	2 – 3	2 – 3
Head of radicchio lettuce (about 10 oz., 285 g), cut or torn	1	1
Fennel bulb (white part only), thinly sliced	1	1
Pine nuts, toasted (see Tip, page 105)	1/2 cup	125 mL

Orange Dressing: Combine first 6 ingredients in jar with tight-fitting lid. Shake well. Makes 1 cup (250 mL) dressing.

Combine raisins and 1/2 of dressing in small bowl. Cover. Let stand for 30 minutes.

Preheat electric grill for 5 minutes or gas barbecue to medium. Place sausages on greased grill. Cook for about 20 minutes, turning occasionally, until browned and no longer pink inside. Cut on diagonal into 1 inch (2.5 cm) pieces.

Combine raisin mixture, sausage and remaining 4 ingredients in large bowl. Drizzle with remaining dressing. Toss until coated. Makes about 10 cups (2.5 L).

1 cup (250 mL): 315 Calories; 24.6 g Total Fat (14.1 g Mono, 3.9 g Poly, 5.3 g Sat); 27 mg Cholesterol; 16 g Carbohydrate; 3 g Fibre; 10 g Protein; 381 mg Sodium

Pictured on page 36.

Barbecued Pork Salad

*Spiced strips of pork combine with a delightful dressing and
fresh salad greens in this crisp, colourful salad.*

Small navel oranges	4	4
Thinly sliced halved red onion	2/3 cup	150 mL
ORANGE DRESSING		
Olive (or cooking) oil	1/3 cup	75 mL
Orange juice	1/4 cup	60 mL
Apple cider vinegar	3 tbsp.	50 mL
Liquid honey	1 tbsp.	15 mL
Grated orange zest	1/2 tsp.	2 mL
Dried sweet basil	1/2 tsp.	2 mL
Salt	1/4 tsp.	1 mL
Garlic powder	1/8 tsp.	0.5 mL
Pepper, sprinkle		
Pork tenderloin, trimmed of fat	1 lb.	454 g
Garlic and herb no-salt seasoning (such as Mrs. Dash)	1 tsp.	5 mL
Pepper, heavy sprinkle		
Cut or torn mixed salad greens	10 cups	2.5 L

Peel oranges. Remove white pith. Slice oranges thinly. Put into large bowl.
Add onion.

Orange Dressing: Process first 9 ingredients in blender for 10 seconds.
Makes 1 cup (250 mL) dressing. Pour over orange mixture. Toss gently to
coat. Chill for 2 hours.

Cut tenderloin almost in half lengthwise, but not quite through, to other
side. Press open to flatten. Sprinkle both sides with seasoning and pepper.
Preheat gas barbecue to medium. Place tenderloin on greased grill. Cook
for 15 to 20 minutes, turning once, until meat thermometer inserted into
thickest part reads 155°F (68°C) or until desired doneness. Cover with foil.
Let stand for 10 minutes. Internal temperature should rise to at least
160°F (70°C).

(continued on next page)

Add salad greens to orange mixture. Toss. Divide among 4 individual salad plates. Cut tenderloin into 1/4 inch (6 mm) thick slices. Arrange several slices of pork in fan shape in centre of each salad. Serve immediately. Makes 4 individual salads.

1 salad: 422 Calories; 20.5 g Total Fat (13.9 g Mono, 1.9 g Poly, 3.4 g Sat); 67 mg Cholesterol; 31 g Carbohydrate; 3 g Fibre; 32 g Protein; 190 mg Sodium

Pictured on page 125.

Warm Potato Salad

A creamy salad with a mild tang. This is a great dish to take to a potluck as it is easy to prepare and suitable for any time of year.

Red baby potatoes with peel (about 2 lbs., 900 g), halved	20	20
Olive (or cooking) oil	1 tbsp.	15 mL
Salt	1/2 tsp.	2 mL
Pepper	1/4 tsp.	1 mL
Bacon slices, cooked crisp and crumbled	10	10
Thinly sliced red onion	1/2 cup	125 mL
Mayonnaise (or salad dressing)	1/2 cup	125 mL
Sour cream	1/3 cup	75 mL
Grainy mustard	3 tbsp.	50 mL
Chopped fresh chives, cut into 1/2 inch (12 mm) pieces	3 tbsp.	50 mL

Put first 4 ingredients into large bowl. Toss until coated. Arrange in single layer on ungreased baking sheet. Bake in 375°F (190°C) oven for about 50 minutes until potatoes are tender and browned. Cool slightly. Return to clean large bowl.

Add bacon and onion.

Combine mayonnaise, sour cream and mustard in small bowl. Add to potato mixture. Toss until coated.

Add chives. Toss. Makes about 6 cups (1.5 L).

1 cup (250 mL): 379 Calories; 23.6 g Total Fat (12.5 g Mono, 6.2 g Poly, 4.1 g Sat); 39 mg Cholesterol; 28 g Carbohydrate; 3 g Fibre; 14 g Protein; 986 mg Sodium

Zesty Potato Salad

A fresh, fattoush-style salad with lots of fresh parsley and mint. This is a nicely textured, colourful combination that your guests will love.

ZESTY DRESSING

Olive (or cooking) oil	3/4 cup	175 mL
Lemon juice	1/2 cup	125 mL
Grainy mustard	1 1/2 tbsp.	25 mL
Finely grated lemon zest	1 tsp.	5 mL
Coarsely ground pepper (or 1/2 tsp., 2 mL, pepper)	1 tsp.	5 mL
Brown sugar, packed	1 tsp.	5 mL
Garlic cloves, minced (or 1/2 tsp., 2 mL, powder)	2	2
Salt	1/4 tsp.	1 mL
Pork tenderloin, trimmed of fat	3/4 lb.	340 g
Red baby potatoes (about 19 oz., 540 g), halved	12	12
Pita breads (8 inch, 20 cm, diameter)	2	2
English cucumbers (with peel), halved lengthwise and thinly sliced	2	2
Coarsely chopped fresh parsley (not dried)	1 1/2 cups	375 mL
Thinly sliced radish	1 cup	250 mL
Coarsely chopped fresh mint leaves (not dried)	2 – 5 tbsp.	30 – 75 mL

Zesty Dressing: Combine first 8 ingredients in jar with tight-fitting lid. Shake well. Makes about 1 1/2 cups (375 mL) dressing.

Put tenderloin into medium bowl. Add 1/3 cup (75 mL) dressing. Turn until coated. Cover. Marinate in refrigerator for 3 to 6 hours. Drain and discard marinade.

Put potatoes and 1 tbsp. (15 mL) dressing into separate medium bowl. Toss until coated. Arrange in single layer on ungreased baking sheet. Bake in 400°F (205°C) oven for about 40 minutes until potatoes are tender and golden.

Place pita breads on separate ungreased baking sheet or directly on oven rack. Bake in 400°F (205°C) oven for about 5 minutes until crisp. Cool. Break into 2 inch (5 cm) pieces. Preheat gas barbecue to low. Place tenderloin on greased grill. Close lid. Cook for about 30 minutes, turning occasionally, until meat thermometer inserted into thickest part reads 155°F (68°C) or until desired doneness. Cover with foil. Let stand for 10 minutes. Internal temperature should rise to at least 160°F (70°C). Cut into 1/4 inch (6 mm) thick slices. Transfer to large bowl.

(continued on next page)

Salads

Add potatoes, remaining 4 ingredients and remaining dressing. Toss until coated. Cover. Chill for 30 minutes. Toss. Add pita pieces. Toss. Serve immediately. Makes 8 cups (2 L).

1 cup (250 mL): 333 Calories; 21.9 g Total Fat (15.3 g Mono, 2.1 g Poly, 3.2 g Sat); 25 mg Cholesterol; 22 g Carbohydrate; 2 g Fibre; 14 g Protein; 225 mg Sodium

Pictured on page 126.

Spinach And Pear Salad

A unique salad flavoured with bacon, blue cheese and pecans.

Bag of fresh spinach, stems removed	6 oz.	170 g
Pecans, toasted (see Tip, page 105) and coarsely chopped	1/2 cup	125 mL
Crumbled blue cheese (about 1 1/4 oz., 35 g)	1/4 cup	60 mL
Bacon slices, cooked crisp and crumbled	8	8
Medium pear, peeled, quartered, cored and thinly sliced	1	1
APPLE CIDER DRESSING		
Olive (or cooking) oil	1/3 cup	75 mL
Apple cider vinegar	2 tbsp.	30 mL
Chopped fresh thyme leaves (or 1/2 tsp., 2 mL, dried)	2 tsp.	10 mL
Brown sugar, packed	2 tsp.	10 mL
Garlic clove, minced (or 1/4 tsp., 1 mL, powder)	1	1
Salt	1/4 tsp.	1 mL

Combine first 5 ingredients in large bowl.

Apple Cider Dressing: Combine all 6 ingredients in jar with tight-fitting lid. Shake well. Makes about 1/2 cup (125 mL) dressing. Drizzle over spinach mixture. Toss gently. Makes about 7 cups (1.75 L).

1 cup (250 mL): 251 Calories; 20.7 g Total Fat (12.3 g Mono, 2.9 g Poly, 4.3 g Sat); 22 mg Cholesterol; 8 g Carbohydrate; 2 g Fibre; 10 g Protein; 624 mg Sodium

Pictured on page 143.

Fancy Curried Pork Salad

This is a great recipe for using up leftover pork. Fresh pineapple halves are generously filled with this chunky salad. The result is unique and eye-catching, and it would work well as a buffet salad.

Fresh pineapple	1	1
Mayonnaise (not salad dressing)	1 cup	250 mL
Half-and-half cream (or homogenized milk)	1/2 cup	125 mL
Hot mango chutney, finely chopped	1/4 cup	60 mL
Minced crystallized ginger	1 tbsp.	15 mL
Curry powder	2 tsp.	10 mL
Celery seed	1/4 tsp.	1 mL
Diced celery	1 cup	250 mL
Diced red onion	1/3 cup	75 mL
Leftover roast pork, cut into 1/2 inch (12 mm) cubes	2 cups	500 mL
Medium avocados, diced	2	2
Macadamia nuts, toasted (see Tip, page 105) and chopped	3/4 cup	175 mL

Cut pineapple in half lengthwise. Cut down through centre core of each half, but not quite through shell. Remove pineapple, leaving 3/4 inch (2 cm) thick shell. Cover shells with plastic wrap. Chill. Cut out and discard core from pineapple. Cut pineapple into 3/4 inch (2 cm) cubes. Set aside.

Put mayonnaise into large bowl. Stir in cream slowly until smooth. Add next 4 ingredients. Stir.

Add pineapple cubes, celery, onion and pork. Stir until coated. Chill for at least 8 hours or overnight.

Fold in avocado. Makes about 7 cups (1.75 L). Spoon into pineapple shells.

Sprinkle with macadamia nuts. Serves 8 to 10 as a side dish.

1 serving: 624 Calories; 47.4 g Total Fat (27.8 g Mono, 9.6 g Poly, 7.8 g Sat); 76 mg Cholesterol; 31 g Carbohydrate; 6 g Fibre; 23 g Protein; 228 mg Sodium

Pictured on page 18 and on back cover.

Tomato And Bacon Sandwiches

These thick, colourful open-faced sandwiches are hearty and filling. Eat them with a knife and fork and enjoy the mouth-watering combination of flavours. Yum!

Roma (plum) tomatoes, halved lengthwise	6	6
Sweet (or regular) chili sauce	1 tbsp.	15 mL
Salt, sprinkle		
Coarsely ground pepper, sprinkle		
Bacon slices	12	12
Sour cream	1/2 cup	125 mL
Sweet (or regular) chili sauce	2 tbsp.	30 mL
French bread slices, cut 1/2 inch (12 mm) thick	4	4
Large avocado, thinly sliced	1	1

Brush cut surfaces of tomatoes with first amount of chili sauce. Place, cut side up, on greased wire rack on baking sheet. Sprinkle with salt and pepper. Bake in 375°F (190°C) oven for about 1 hour until tomatoes are wilted.

Cook bacon in frying pan on medium for 5 to 7 minutes, until browned and almost crisp. Remove to paper towels to drain.

Combine sour cream and second amount of chili sauce in small bowl.

Divide and spread sour cream mixture onto 1 side of each bread slice. Top each with 1/4 of avocado, 3 bacon slices halved crosswise and 3 tomato halves. Serve immediately. Makes 4 sandwiches.

1 sandwich: 326 Calories; 18.7 g Total Fat (9.1 g Mono, 2 g Poly, 6 g Sat); 52 mg Cholesterol; 20 g Carbohydrate; 4 g Fibre; 21 g Protein; 1258 mg Sodium

Pictured on page 53.

Fruited Calzones

These large, warm pockets are filled with the flavours of apple,
pork and mozzarella cheese. The whole family will enjoy these.
Kal-ZOH-nays are fun to eat and delicious!

CALZONE DOUGH

All-purpose flour	2 cups	500 mL
Instant yeast	2 tsp.	10 mL
Salt	1/2 tsp.	2 mL
Hot water	2/3 cup	150 mL
Granulated sugar	1/2 tsp.	2 mL
Cooking oil	2 tbsp.	30 mL

FILLING

Cooking oil	2 tsp.	10 mL
Pork tenderloin, cut into thin strips	3/4 lb.	340 g
Medium cooking apple (such as McIntosh), peeled and sliced	1	1
Brown sugar, packed	2 tbsp.	30 mL
Water	1 tbsp.	15 mL
Water	1/4 cup	60 mL
All-purpose flour	1 tbsp.	15 mL
White vinegar	1 tsp.	5 mL
Salt	1/4 tsp.	1 mL
Pepper	1/8 tsp.	0.5 mL
Raisins	1 tbsp.	15 mL
Applesauce	1/4 cup	60 mL
Grated part-skim mozzarella cheese	1 1/3 cups	325 mL

CALZONE DOUGH:

Food Processor Method: Put flour, yeast and salt into food processor fitted with dough blade. Stir water and sugar in liquid measure until dissolved. Add cooking oil. With motor running, slowly pour mixture through feed chute. Process for 50 to 60 seconds. If dough seems sticky, add about 1/2 tsp. (2 mL) flour.

(continued on next page)

Hand Method: Combine flour, yeast and salt in medium bowl. Make a well in centre. Stir water and sugar in liquid measure until dissolved. Add cooking oil. Pour mixture into well. Mix until dough pulls away from side of bowl and is no longer sticky. Knead on lightly floured surface for 5 to 8 minutes until smooth and elastic. Divide dough into 4 equal balls. Cover with greased waxed paper.

Filling: Heat cooking oil in medium frying pan on medium-high. Add pork. Cook for 1 to 2 minutes until no longer pink. Transfer to medium bowl.

Put apple, brown sugar and first amount of water into same frying pan. Stir. Cover. Cook on medium-low for about 2 minutes, stirring occasionally, until apple is tender.

Combine next 5 ingredients in small bowl until smooth. Add raisins. Stir. Add to apple mixture. Heat and stir for about 2 minutes until boiling and thickened. Remove from heat. Add pork. Stir.

Roll out 1 dough ball into 8 inch (20 cm) circle. Spread with 1 tbsp. (15 mL) applesauce, leaving 1 inch (2.5 cm) border. Spoon 1/4 of filling (generous 1/3 cup, 75 mL) onto 1 side of centre.

Sprinkle with 1/3 cup (75 mL) cheese. Dampen edge of dough with water. Fold dough over filling. Fold edge up and over to seal. Press rounded edge firmly with fork. Repeat with remaining dough, applesauce, filling and cheese. Arrange on large greased baking sheet. Poke holes in tops with fork to allow steam to escape. Bake on bottom rack in 425°F (220°C) oven for about 15 minutes until golden brown. Makes 4 calzones.

1 calzone: 615 Calories; 18.6 g Total Fat (8.3 g Mono, 3.5 g Poly, 5.6 g Sat); 73 mg Cholesterol; 72 g Carbohydrate; 3 g Fibre; 38 g Protein; 635 mg Sodium

Pictured on page 89.

Variation: Omit applesauce. Use same amount of chutney, salsa or pizza sauce.

Always remember to keep fresh meat cold. If the weather is warm, transport your meat from the grocery store to home in your air-conditioned car rather than in the trunk. If your drive home is longer than 30 minutes, bring a cooler to transport your meat. As soon as you get home, place the meat on a tray in the coldest part of the refrigerator or in the meat compartment. Use ground pork within 24 hours and chops, steaks and roasts within 2 to 4 days. Cured and smoked products will keep for up to 1 week. If meat will not be used within these time ranges, store it in the freezer.

Bacon And Egg Sandwich

An excellent sandwich stuffed with lots of bacon and cheese.
This is a great way to use up leftover bacon.

Bacon slices	4	4
Large egg	1	1
Water	1 tbsp.	15 mL
Pepper, sprinkle		
Grated medium Cheddar cheese	1/4 cup	60 mL
Bread slices, toasted (buttered, optional)	2	2

Cook bacon in frying pan on medium for about 10 minutes until crisp. Remove to paper towels to drain. Drain and discard all but 2 tsp. (10 mL) drippings. Crumble bacon into small bowl.

Add egg, water and pepper. Beat with fork. Add mixture to reserved drippings. Cook on medium-low for about 5 minutes, pushing egg towards centre of pan to shape into size of bread slice, until set.

Sprinkle 1/2 of cheese over 1 bread slice. Cover with egg mixture. Sprinkle with remaining cheese. Top with remaining bread slice. Makes 1 sandwich.

1 sandwich: 601 Calories; 24.6 g Total Fat (9 g Mono, 3 g Poly, 10.6 g Sat); 270 mg Cholesterol; 49 g Carbohydrate; 2 g Fibre; 43 g Protein; 1973 mg Sodium

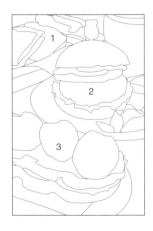

Sandwiches

Grilled Ham And Cheese Sandwiches

These crispy grilled sandwiches take no time at all to prepare.
The kids will love this dressed-up version of your basic grilled cheese.

Hard margarine (or butter), softened	3 tbsp.	50 mL
Dijon mustard	1 tbsp.	15 mL
Worcestershire sauce	2 tsp.	10 mL
Onion flakes	2 tsp.	10 mL
French bread slices, cut 1/4 inch (6 mm) thick	8	8
Cooked ham slices	8	8
Swiss cheese slices	4	4

Combine first 4 ingredients in small bowl.

Spread margarine mixture onto 1 side of each bread slice.

Top unbuttered sides of 4 bread slices with 2 ham slices and 1 cheese slice. Top with remaining bread slices, buttered side up. Preheat 2-sided electric grill for 5 minutes. Place sandwiches on lightly greased grill. Close lid. Cook for about 5 minutes until golden. Makes 4 sandwiches.

1 sandwich: 299 Calories; 14.9 g Total Fat (4.6 g Mono, 0.9 g Poly, 8.4 g Sat); 53 mg Cholesterol; 26 g Carbohydrate; 2 g Fibre; 15 g Protein; 754 mg Sodium

Pictured on page 53.

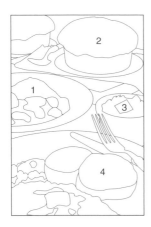

1. Pork Stew And Dumplings, page 64
2. Creamy Pork Pies, page 66
3. Green Tomato Pickle, page 146
4. Glazed Meatloaf, page 87

Props Courtesy Of: Casa Bugatti

Polynesian Burgers

These large, highly seasoned patties can be
topped with your choice of condiments. Delicious!

Lean ground pork	2 lbs.	900 g
Fine dry bread crumbs	2/3 cup	150 mL
Salt	1 tsp.	5 mL
Dried thyme leaves	1/2 tsp.	2 mL
Ground ginger	1/2 tsp.	2 mL
Pepper	1/4 tsp.	1 mL
Cayenne pepper	1/4 tsp.	1 mL
Large eggs	2	2
Green onions, finely chopped	3	3
Garlic cloves, minced (or 1/2 tsp., 2 mL, powder)	2	2
Thick teriyaki basting sauce	2 tbsp.	30 mL
Dry sherry	1 tbsp.	15 mL
Large hamburger buns, split	8	8

CONDIMENTS (optional)
Fresh bean sprouts
Jalapeño pepper jelly
Mayonnaise (or salad dressing)
Pineapple slices (grilled if desired)
Shredded lettuce (your choice)
Teriyaki sauce
Thinly sliced red or green pepper

Combine first 7 ingredients in large bowl.

Beat eggs with fork in small bowl. Add next 4 ingredients. Stir. Add to ground pork mixture. Mix well. Divide and shape into 8 patties, about 4 inches (10 cm) in diameter. Chill until ready to cook. Broil on greased broiler pan on centre rack in oven for about 8 minutes per side, or cook on lightly greased electric grill for about 5 minutes per side, until no pink remains.

Place patties on bottom bun halves.

Condiments: Top with desired condiments and remaining bun halves. Makes 8 burgers.

1 patty with bun: 427 Calories; 20.8 g Total Fat (8.5 g Mono, 2.9 g Poly, 6.8 g Sat); 103 mg Cholesterol; 29 g Carbohydrate; 2 g Fibre; 28 g Protein; 800 mg Sodium

Pictured on page 53.

Mexican Sausage Burgers

These meaty patties are so easy to make. Top with your
choice of condiments for a personalized flavour.

Lean ground pork	2 lbs.	900 g
White vinegar	1/4 cup	60 mL
Chili powder	1 tbsp.	15 mL
Salt	2 tsp.	10 mL
Dried whole oregano	1 1/2 tsp.	7 mL
Garlic powder	1/4 tsp.	1 mL
Pepper	1/4 tsp.	1 mL
Hamburger buns, split	8	8

CONDIMENTS (optional)
Salsa
Shredded lettuce
Sliced tomato
Chopped red onion
Sour cream

Combine first 7 ingredients in large bowl. Cover with plastic wrap. Chill for at least 24 hours to blend flavours. Divide and shape into 8 patties, about 4 inches (10 cm) in diameter. Preheat gas barbecue to medium. Cook patties on greased grill for 3 1/2 to 4 minutes per side, or cook in greased non-stick frying pan on medium for 2 1/2 to 3 minutes per side, until browned and no pink remains.

Place patties on bottom bun halves.

Condiments: Top with desired condiments and remaining bun halves. Makes 8 burgers.

1 patty with bun: 372 Calories; 19.3 g Total Fat (7.8 g Mono, 2.7 g Poly, 6.3 g Sat); 56 mg Cholesterol; 23 g Carbohydrate; 2 g Fibre; 25 g Protein; 840 mg Sodium

Apple Smoked Cheese Ciabatta

These tempting open-faced sandwiches are visually appealing and delicious! This is a great way to use up leftover roast pork.

Olive (or cooking) oil	1 tbsp.	15 mL
Thinly sliced onion	2 cups	500 mL
Applesauce	2 tbsp.	30 mL
Red wine vinegar	1 tbsp.	15 mL
Salt, sprinkle		
Pepper, sprinkle		
Ciabatta bread loaf (with Asiago cheese), 9 inch (22 cm) length	1	1
Hard margarine (or butter), melted	3 tbsp.	50 mL
Small cooking apple (such as McIntosh), peeled and thinly sliced	1	1
Cooked pork slices, cut in half	8	8
Coarsely grated smoked applewood cheese	1 1/2 cups	375 mL

Heat olive oil in frying pan on medium. Add onion. Cook for 5 to 10 minutes, stirring often, until soft and lightly browned.

Add next 4 ingredients. Heat and stir for about 1 minute until vinegar is evaporated. Set aside.

Cut ends from bread loaf. Cut bread into sixteen 1/2 inch (12 mm) slices. Brush 1 side of each slice with margarine. Place slices, buttered side up, on lightly greased baking sheet with sides. Broil on top rack in oven for about 3 minutes until lightly browned.

Divide and layer onion mixture, apple and pork on unbuttered side of each bread slice. Sprinkle each with cheese. Broil on top rack in oven for about 3 minutes until lightly browned and cheese is bubbling. Makes 16 sandwiches.

1 sandwich: 111 Calories; 6.3 g Total Fat (2.3 g Mono, 0.3 g Poly, 3.2 g Sat); 26 mg Cholesterol; 6 g Carbohydrate; 1 g Fibre; 8 g Protein; 115 mg Sodium

Oven-Baked Ham Sandwiches

These inviting, cheesy sandwiches are a cross between French toast and a ham and cheese sandwich. Cut each sandwich into quarters to make a filling snack for a group of kids.

Whole wheat bread slices	4	4
Salad dressing (or mayonnaise)	1 tbsp.	15 mL
Dijon (or spicy) mustard	1 tbsp.	15 mL
Cooked ham slices (about 2 1/4 oz., 63 g)	4	4
Large egg	1	1
Water	1 tbsp.	15 mL
Salt	1/4 tsp.	1 mL
Grated sharp (or medium) Cheddar cheese	1/2 cup	125 mL
Paprika, sprinkle		

Divide and spread 1 side of 2 bread slices with salad dressing and 1 side of 2 bread slices with mustard.

Place 2 ham slices on each mustard-coated bread slice. Top with remaining bread slices.

Beat egg, water and salt with fork in pie plate or shallow dish. Dip sandwiches, 1 at a time, until both sides are coated. Place on greased baking sheet.

Sprinkle with cheese and paprika. Bake on bottom rack in 400°F (205°C) oven for 10 to 15 minutes until bottom is browned. Makes 2 sandwiches.

1 sandwich: 390 Calories; 22.1 g Total Fat (8.9 g Mono, 3.3 g Poly, 8.6 g Sat); 145 mg Cholesterol; 28 g Carbohydrate; 4 g Fibre; 22 g Protein; 1222 mg Sodium

---

Paré Pointer
The invisible man has a mirror to see if he isn't there.

One-Dish Ham Dinner

This is a colourful vegetable and noodle dish with a
wonderful golden crumb topping. The entire family will love it!

Medium egg noodles	8 oz.	225 g
Boiling water	12 cups	3 L
Salt	1 tbsp.	15 mL
Frozen Oriental mixed vegetables, thawed and drained	4 cups	1 L
Milk	1 1/2 cups	375 mL
All-purpose flour	3 tbsp.	50 mL
Seasoned salt	1 tsp.	5 mL
Pepper	1/4 tsp.	1 mL
Onion powder	1/4 tsp.	1 mL
Grated sharp Cheddar cheese	2 cups	500 mL
Diced cooked ham (about 10 oz., 285 g)	2 cups	500 mL
Prepared horseradish	4 tsp.	20 mL
TOPPING		
Hard margarine (or butter)	1/4 cup	60 mL
Fine dry bread crumbs	2/3 cup	150 mL

Cook noodles in boiling water and salt in large uncovered pot or Dutch oven for 5 to 7 minutes until tender but firm. Drain. Return to pot.

Add vegetables. Stir.

Combine next 5 ingredients with whisk in medium saucepan until smooth. Heat and stir on medium until boiling and thickened. Remove from heat.

Add cheese. Stir until melted. Add ham and horseradish. Stir. Add to noodle mixture. Stir gently. Turn into ungreased 3 quart (3 L) casserole.

Topping: Melt margarine in small saucepan. Add bread crumbs. Stir until well mixed. Sprinkle over noodle mixture. Bake, uncovered, in 350°F (175°C) oven for about 30 minutes until heated through. Makes about 9 cups (2.25 L). Serves 6.

1 serving: 598 Calories; 26.7 g Total Fat (8.1 g Mono, 1.6 g Poly, 15 g Sat); 130 mg Cholesterol; 60 g Carbohydrate; 5 g Fibre; 31 g Protein; 2242 mg Sodium

Variation: Add 1 cup (250 mL) frozen kernel corn, thawed and drained, or canned kernel corn, drained.

Apple Pork Casserole

This rich brown, saucy stew can be served with couscous,
rice or pasta. Its aroma is warm and inviting.

Cooking oil	1 tbsp.	15 mL
Boneless inside pork leg roast, cut into 1 inch (2.5 cm) cubes	1 1/2 lbs.	680 g
Cooking oil	1 tbsp.	15 mL
Medium onions, quartered	2	2
Garlic cloves, minced (or 1 tsp., 5 mL, powder)	4	4
Ground ginger	1 tsp.	5 mL
Paprika	1 tsp.	5 mL
Cinnamon stick (4 inch, 10 cm, length)	1	1
Prepared chicken broth	2 cups	500 mL
Tomato paste	1/4 cup	60 mL
Salt	1/4 tsp.	1 mL
Tart medium cooking apples (such as Granny Smith), peeled, cored and cut into 8 wedges each	4	4
Lemon juice	2 tbsp.	30 mL
Liquid honey	2 tbsp.	30 mL

Heat first amount of cooking oil in large ovenproof pot or Dutch oven on medium-high. Cook pork, in batches, for about 5 minutes, stirring occasionally, until browned. Remove from pot.

Heat second amount of cooking oil in same pot on medium-low. Add onion and garlic. Cook for about 10 minutes, stirring occasionally, until onion is softened.

Add ginger, paprika and cinnamon stick. Heat and stir for about 1 minute until fragrant.

Add pork, broth, tomato paste and salt. Stir. Cover. Bake in 325°F (160°C) oven for 1 1/2 hours.

Add apple. Stir. Bake, uncovered, for about 40 minutes until apple is soft and sauce is slightly thickened.

Remove and discard cinnamon stick. Add lemon juice and honey. Stir. Makes about 7 cups (1.75 L). Serves 6.

1 serving: 297 Calories; 9.4 g Total Fat (4.6 g Mono, 2 g Poly, 1.8 g Sat); 91 mg Cholesterol; 27 g Carbohydrate; 3 g Fibre; 27 g Protein; 426 mg Sodium

Half-The-Time Cassoulet

This is similar to a French cassoulet, but it can be prepared in less than half the time! This hearty wintertime stew is brimming with beans and meat. Serve it in bowls with a hearty grain bread for dipping.

Olive (or cooking) oil	2 tbsp.	30 mL
Boneless pork loin, trimmed of fat and cut into 3/4 inch (2 cm) cubes	1 1/2 lbs.	680 g
Diced onion	2/3 cup	150 mL
Garlic cloves, minced (or 3/4 tsp., 4 mL, powder)	3	3
All-purpose flour	2 tbsp.	30 mL
Seasoned salt	1 tsp.	5 mL
Pepper	1/4 tsp.	1 mL
Cayenne pepper	1/8 tsp.	0.5 mL
Can of condensed chicken broth	10 oz.	284 mL
Can of tomato sauce	7 1/2 oz.	213 mL
Dry white (or alcohol-free) wine	1/4 cup	60 mL
Bay leaf	1	1
Cans of white kidney beans (19 oz., 540 mL, each) or other white beans, rinsed and drained	3	3
Diced garlic ham sausage (or other cooked spicy sausage)	12 oz.	340 g
Chopped fresh parsley (or 3/4 tsp., 4 mL, flakes)	1 tbsp.	15 mL
Chopped fresh thyme leaves (or 1/2 tsp., 2 mL, dried)	2 tsp.	10 mL

Heat olive oil in large pot or Dutch oven on medium-high. Add pork, onion and garlic. Heat and stir for 3 to 4 minutes until pork is starting to brown.

Add next 4 ingredients. Heat and stir for 3 to 4 minutes until flour is starting to brown.

Add broth, tomato sauce, wine and bay leaf. Stir, scraping up any brown bits from bottom of pan. Heat and stir until boiling and thickened. Reduce heat to medium-low. Simmer, uncovered, for about 30 minutes, stirring occasionally, until slightly reduced.

(continued on next page)

Add remaining 4 ingredients. Stir. Cover. Cook on low for about 30 minutes, stirring several times, until heated through. Remove and discard bay leaf. Makes 10 cups (2.5 L).

1 cup (250 mL): 404 Calories; 14.9 g Total Fat (7.4 g Mono, 2 g Poly, 4.5 g Sat); 74 mg Cholesterol; 33 g Carbohydrate; 1 g Fibre; 33 g Protein; 1279 mg Sodium

Ham Casserole

Pink cubes of ham, bright green peas and tender noodles combine in this creamy casserole. This is an excellent dish to make ahead.

Medium egg noodles	8 oz.	225 g
Boiling water	12 cups	3 L
Salt	2 tsp.	10 mL
Frozen peas	2 cups	500 mL
Cubed (or chopped) cooked ham	1 1/2 cups	375 mL
Can of condensed cream of mushroom soup	10 oz.	284 mL
Milk	1/2 cup	125 mL
Grated sharp Cheddar cheese	1/2 cup	125 mL
Prepared mustard	1 tsp.	5 mL
Worcestershire sauce	1/2 tsp.	2 mL
Onion powder	1/4 tsp.	1 mL
TOPPING		
Hard margarine (or butter)	2 tbsp.	30 mL
Fine dry bread crumbs	1/3 cup	75 mL
Grated sharp Cheddar cheese	1/3 cup	75 mL

Cook noodles in boiling water and salt in large uncovered pot or Dutch oven for 5 to 7 minutes until tender but firm. Drain.

Combine next 8 ingredients in large bowl. Add noodles. Stir. Turn into ungreased 3 quart (3 L) casserole.

Topping: Melt margarine in small saucepan. Add bread crumbs and cheese. Stir until well mixed. Sprinkle over noodle mixture. Bake, uncovered, in 350°F (175°C) oven for about 45 minutes until heated through. Serves 6.

1 serving: 411 Calories; 17.3 g Total Fat (5 g Mono, 2.9 g Poly, 8 g Sat); 86 mg Cholesterol; 43 g Carbohydrate; 4 g Fibre; 20 g Protein; 1837 mg Sodium

Pork Stew And Dumplings

What could be better on a cold day than a warm, homey stew?
The soft, cheesy dumplings are a wonderful addition to this recipe.

All-purpose flour	3 tbsp.	50 mL
Pepper	1/2 tsp.	2 mL
Boneless pork shoulder butt roast, trimmed of fat and cut into 1 inch (2.5 cm) cubes	2 lbs.	900 g
Cooking oil	2 tbsp.	30 mL
Prepared chicken broth	4 cups	1 L
Medium onions, halved and sliced	2	2
Medium potatoes, cut into 1/2 inch (12 mm) thick slices	2	2
Medium carrots, cut into 1/2 inch (12 mm) thick slices	2	2
Fresh (or frozen, thawed) peas	1 cup	250 mL
Salt	1/2 tsp.	2 mL
DUMPLINGS		
All-purpose flour	1 cup	250 mL
Baking powder	2 tsp.	10 mL
Salt, just a pinch		
Hard margarine (or butter), cut up	1/4 cup	60 mL
Chopped fresh parsley (or 3/4 tsp., 4 mL, flakes)	1 tbsp.	15 mL
Grated sharp white Cheddar cheese	1/2 cup	125 mL
Buttermilk (or reconstituted from powder)	1/3 cup	75 mL
Large egg	1	1

Combine flour and pepper in large bowl or resealable freezer bag. Add pork in 2 batches. Cover or seal. Toss until coated.

Heat cooking oil in large pot or Dutch oven on medium-high. Cook pork, in 2 batches, for 5 to 10 minutes, stirring occasionally, until browned.

Add next 6 ingredients. Bring to a boil. Reduce heat to medium-low. Cover. Simmer for about 1 1/2 hours, stirring occasionally, until pork is tender.

Dumplings: Combine flour, baking powder and salt in medium bowl. Cut in margarine until crumbly.

Add parsley and cheese. Mix well.

(continued on next page)

Casseroles & Stews

Combine buttermilk and egg in 1 cup (250 mL) liquid measure. Add to flour mixture. Mix until soft and sticky dough forms. Drop by rounded tablespoonfuls into vegetable mixture, 1/4 to 1/2 inch (6 to 12 mm) apart. Makes about 15 dumplings. Cover. Simmer for 15 to 20 minutes until dumplings are firm. Serves 8.

1 serving: 437 Calories; 20.9 g Total Fat (8.4 g Mono, 2.5 g Poly, 8.5 g Sat); 121 mg Cholesterol; 28 g Carbohydrate; 2 g Fibre; 33 g Protein; 826 mg Sodium

Pictured on page 54.

Sweet And Spicy Casserole

This sweet and spicy dish is perfect for a large group.

All-purpose flour	1/4 cup	60 mL
Granulated sugar	2 tbsp.	30 mL
Boneless pork shoulder butt roast, trimmed of fat and cut into 3/4 inch (2 cm) cubes	4 1/2 lbs.	2 kg
Cooking oil	2 tbsp.	30 mL
Cooking oil	1 tbsp.	15 mL
Thinly sliced onion	2 cups	500 mL
Medium carrots, cut into 1/4 inch (6 mm) thick slices	3	3
Medium potatoes, cut into 1/4 inch (6 mm) thick slices	3	3
Ketchup	1/3 cup	75 mL
Water	1/3 cup	75 mL
Malt vinegar	1/4 cup	60 mL
Worcestershire sauce	3 tbsp.	50 mL

Combine flour and sugar in large bowl or resealable freezer bag. Add pork in batches. Cover or seal. Toss until coated.

Heat first amount of cooking oil in large frying pan on medium-high. Cook pork, in batches, for about 5 minutes, stirring often, until browned. Remove from pan.

Heat second amount of cooking oil in same frying pan on medium-low. Add onion. Cook for 5 to 10 minutes, stirring occasionally, until softened.

Combine pork, onion, carrot and potato in greased 4 quart (4 L) casserole.

Combine remaining 4 ingredients in small bowl. Pour over pork mixture. Cover. Bake in 350°F (175°C) oven for 2 hours. Stir. Bake, uncovered, for 20 to 30 minutes until sauce is thickened and pork is tender. Makes about 11 cups (2.75 L). Serves 8.

1 serving: 533 Calories; 21.9 g Total Fat (10.5 g Mono, 3.4 g Poly, 6.1 g Sat); 158 mg Cholesterol; 26 g Carbohydrate; 3 g Fibre; 56 g Protein; 381 mg Sodium

Creamy Pork Pies

A savoury combination of pork, vegetables and gravy is covered with a flaky, golden pastry dome. These warm, rustic pies are perfect for a cold winter evening. Cut the pastry out freehand and don't worry about making the perfect circle.

All-purpose flour	1/3 cup	75 mL
Salt	1/2 tsp.	2 mL
Pepper	1/4 tsp.	1 mL
Boneless pork inside leg roast, cut into 1 inch (2.5 cm) cubes	1 3/4 lbs.	790 g
Cooking oil	3 tbsp.	50 mL
Hard margarine (or butter)	1 tbsp.	15 mL
Medium leek (white and tender green parts only), thinly sliced	1	1
Garlic cloves, minced (or 1/2 tsp., 2 mL, powder)	2	2
Diced carrot	1 cup	250 mL
Finely chopped celery	1/2 cup	125 mL
Dry white (or alcohol-free) wine	1 cup	250 mL
Prepared chicken broth	1 cup	250 mL
Frozen peas	1 cup	250 mL
Sour cream	1/4 cup	60 mL
Liquid honey	1 tbsp.	15 mL
Chopped fresh thyme leaves (or 1/2 tsp., 2 mL, dried)	2 tsp.	10 mL
Salt, just a pinch		
Package of frozen puff pastry, thawed according to package directions	14 oz.	397 g
Large egg, fork-beaten	1	1

Combine flour, first amount of salt and pepper in large resealable freezer bag. Add pork. Seal. Toss until coated.

Heat cooking oil in large pot or Dutch oven on medium-high. Cook pork, in 2 batches, for about 5 minutes, stirring occasionally, until browned. Remove from pot.

Melt margarine in same pot on medium. Add next 4 ingredients. Cook for 5 to 10 minutes, stirring occasionally, until leek is soft.

Add pork, wine and broth. Stir. Bring to a boil. Reduce heat to medium-low. Cover. Simmer for about 1 hour until pork is tender.

(continued on next page)

Add next 5 ingredients. Heat and stir for about 5 minutes until peas are hot. Divide mixture among four 2 cup (500 mL) ramekins.

Roll out each pastry half to 6 1/2 × 13 inch (16.5 × 33 cm) rectangle. Cut each rectangle in half. Trim corners to make 4 circles.

Brush outside edge of circles with egg. Place 1 circle, egg-side down, over each ramekin. Press edge against ramekin to seal. Brush top of pastry with egg. Bake in 400°F (205°C) oven for about 25 minutes until puffy and golden brown. Makes 4 pork pies.

1 pork pie: 1128 Calories; 62.8 g Total Fat (33.3 g Mono, 9.6 g Poly, 16.3 g Sat); 220 mg Cholesterol; 73 g Carbohydrate; 5 g Fibre; 57 g Protein; 924 mg Sodium

Pictured on page 54.

Pork Rice Bake

These tender pork steaks are baked on a bed of rice and seasoned with garlic, thyme and oregano. Make this ahead of time and reheat it for a quick, easy dinner.

Bone-in pork shoulder butt steaks (about 3 lbs., 1.4 kg)	6	6
Garlic salt	1/4 tsp.	1 mL
Pepper, sprinkle		
Hard margarine (or butter)	2 tbsp.	30 mL
Uncooked long grain white rice	1 1/2 cups	375 mL
Dried thyme	3/4 tsp.	4 mL
Dried whole oregano	3/4 tsp.	4 mL
Salt	1/2 tsp.	2 mL
Pepper	1/8 tsp.	0.5 mL
Prepared beef broth	3 cups	750 mL

Sprinkle both sides of steaks with garlic salt and pepper.

Melt margarine in large frying pan on medium. Cook steaks, in batches, for about 2 minutes per side until browned.

Pour rice into greased 9 × 13 inch (22 × 33 cm) pan. Sprinkle with next 4 ingredients. Arrange steaks in single layer over rice.

Pour broth over top. Cover tightly with foil. Bake in 350°F (175°C) oven for about 1 1/2 hours until steaks are tender and all liquid is absorbed. Serves 6.

1 serving: 583 Calories; 23 g Total Fat (9.7 g Mono, 2.2 g Poly, 9 g Sat); 171 mg Cholesterol; 41 g Carbohydrate; 1 g Fibre; 49 g Protein; 1023 mg Sodium

Tomato Pork Curry

This rich stew contains a wonderful variety of spices. The Banana Raita (pronounced RI-tah) can be served on the side to cool your palate.

Cooking oil	1 tbsp.	15 mL
Boneless pork shoulder butt roast, trimmed of fat and cut into 1 inch (2.5 cm) cubes	2 lbs.	900 g
Cooking oil	2 tsp.	10 mL
Chopped onion	1 1/2 cups	375 mL
Garlic cloves, minced (or 1/2 tsp., 2 mL, powder)	2	2
Small fresh red chilies (such as Thai), chopped	2	2
Curry powder	1 tbsp.	15 mL
Cinnamon stick (4 inch, 10 cm, length)	1	1
Can of tomato sauce	14 oz.	398 mL
Medium tomatoes, peeled and coarsely chopped	4	4
Brown sugar, packed	2 tsp.	10 mL
Salt	1 tsp.	5 mL
Plain yogurt	1 cup	250 mL
BANANA RAITA		
Plain yogurt	3/4 cup	175 mL
Mashed banana	3/4 cup	175 mL
Cashews, toasted (see Tip, page 105) and chopped	1/2 cup	125 mL

Heat first amount of cooking oil in large pot or Dutch oven on medium-high. Cook pork, in 2 batches, for 5 to 10 minutes, stirring often, until browned. Transfer to bowl.

Heat second amount of cooking oil in same pot on medium. Add onion, garlic and chilies. Cook for 5 to 10 minutes, stirring often, until softened.

Add curry powder and cinnamon stick. Heat and stir for 1 to 2 minutes until fragrant.

Add pork and next 4 ingredients. Stir. Bring to a boil. Reduce heat to medium-low. Cover. Simmer for about 1 1/2 hours until pork is tender. Remove from heat. Remove and discard cinnamon stick.

Add yogurt. Stir to combine.

Banana Raita: Combine yogurt, banana and cashews in small bowl. Chill for 20 to 30 minutes before serving. Makes about 1 2/3 cups (400 mL) raita. Serve with Tomato Pork Curry. Serves 6.

(continued on next page)

1 serving: 477 Calories; 21.3 g Total Fat (10.5 g Mono, 3.4 g Poly, 5.7 g Sat); 99 mg Cholesterol; 33 g Carbohydrate; 4 g Fibre; 40 g Protein; 978 mg Sodium

Pictured on page 89.

Baked Apricot Onion Steaks

These golden brown steaks are flavoured with a sweet apricot nectar.
The saucy gravy goes well with buttered pasta or roasted potatoes.

Cooking oil	1 tbsp.	15 mL
Bone-in pork shoulder butt steaks (3/4 inch, 2 cm, thick), about 3 lbs. (1.4 kg)	6	6
Cooking oil	1 tbsp.	15 mL
Medium onions, quartered	3	3
Garlic cloves, minced (or 1/2 tsp., 2 mL, powder)	2	2
Medium leek (white and tender green parts only), thinly sliced	1	1
Apricot nectar	2 cups	500 mL
Dry onion soup mix, stir before measuring	2 1/2 tbsp.	37 mL
Chopped fresh parsley (or 1 tbsp., 15 mL, flakes)	1/4 cup	60 mL

Heat first amount of cooking oil in large frying pan on medium-high. Cook steaks, in 2 batches, for about 2 minutes per side until browned. Turn into greased 4 quart (4 L) casserole.

Heat second amount of cooking oil in same frying pan on medium. Add onion, garlic and leek. Cook for 5 to 10 minutes, stirring often, until onion is soft and golden.

Add nectar and soup mix. Stir well. Pour over steaks. Turn until coated. Cover. Bake in 350°F (175°C) oven for 1 hour. Remove cover. Bake for about 45 minutes until steaks are tender and sauce is thickened.

Add parsley. Stir. Serves 6.

1 serving: 299 Calories; 12.8 g Total Fat (6.3 g Mono, 2.3 g Poly, 3.1 g Sat); 76 mg Cholesterol; 19 g Carbohydrate; 2 g Fibre; 27 g Protein; 116 mg Sodium

Pictured on page 72.

Parmesan-Crumbed Chops

These tender, juicy pork chops are coated with a wonderful basil and Parmesan cheese crust. The aroma is warm and very inviting.

Fresh bread crumbs	2 cups	500 mL
Finely grated fresh Parmesan cheese	2/3 cup	150 mL
Finely chopped fresh sweet basil (or 2 tbsp., 30 mL, dried)	1/2 cup	125 mL
Dry mustard	1 tsp.	5 mL
Lemon pepper	1 tsp.	5 mL
All-purpose flour	1/3 cup	75 mL
Large eggs	2	2
Milk	1 tbsp.	15 mL
Loin rib end roast rack, cut into 1-bone portions	3 lbs.	1.4 kg
Cooking oil	1/4 cup	60 mL

Combine first 5 ingredients in shallow dish.

Measure flour onto sheet of waxed paper. Beat eggs and milk with fork in separate shallow dish. Dredge chops in flour. Dip into egg mixture. Press into bread crumb mixture until coated.

Heat cooking oil in large frying pan on medium-low. Add chops. Cook for 8 to 10 minutes per side until tender and golden brown. Serves 6.

1 serving: 764 Calories; 37.6 g Total Fat (17.5 g Mono, 6.2 g Poly, 10.8 g Sat); 224 mg Cholesterol; 39 g Carbohydrate; 6 g Fibre; 65 g Protein; 707 mg Sodium

Pictured on page 36.

1. Polenta-Stuffed Loin, page 102
2. Italian Sausage With Rice, page 94

Props Courtesy Of: Casa Bugatti
Mikasa Home Store

Pork Chop Dinner

This hearty helping of chops and potatoes rests in a warm,
creamy sauce. This recipe works very well in an electric frying pan.
Serve with a salad or cooked vegetables for a complete meal.

Cooking oil	1 tbsp.	15 mL
Bone-in pork chops (about 1 1/2 lbs., 680 g), trimmed of fat	4	4
Sliced fresh white mushrooms	3 cups	750 mL
Baby potatoes (about 1 1/4 lbs., 560 g)	20	20
Light sour cream	1 1/3 cups	325 mL
Dill weed	1 1/2 tsp.	7 mL
Seasoned salt	1/2 tsp.	2 mL

Heat cooking oil in large deep or electric frying pan on medium-high. Add chops. Cook for about 2 minutes per side until browned.

Sprinkle with mushrooms. Arrange potatoes around edge of pan. Reduce heat to medium-low. Cover. Cook for about 30 minutes until potatoes are tender.

Combine sour cream, dill weed and seasoned salt in small bowl. Pour over chops and potatoes. Turn chops. Stir sour cream mixture until combined. Cover. Heat for about 5 minutes until heated through. Serves 4.

1 serving: 429 Calories; 15.6 g Total Fat (4.8 g Mono, 1.8 g Poly, 2.4 g Sat); 117 mg Cholesterol; 25 g Carbohydrate; 5 g Fibre; 47 g Protein; 319 mg Sodium

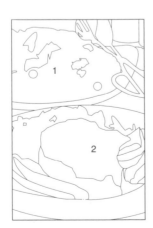

1. Sweet Cabbage Salad, page 42
2. Baked Apricot Onion Steaks, page 69

Props Courtesy Of: Browne & Co. Ltd.
Linens 'N Things

Roasted Pork Chops

The warm flavours in this rustic-looking dish complement each other perfectly. Serve with Peach Chutney, page 141.

Lemon juice	1/3 cup	75 mL
Thinly peeled lemon zest pieces (about 2 inch, 5 cm, lengths)	3	3
Coarsely chopped fresh rosemary (or 1 1/2 tsp., 7 mL, dried)	2 tbsp.	30 mL
Olive (or cooking) oil	2 tbsp.	30 mL
Brown sugar, packed	2 tbsp.	30 mL
Garlic cloves (with peel), bruised	6	6
Coarsely ground pepper (or 1/2 tsp., 2 mL, pepper)	1 tsp.	5 mL
Bone-in pork loin rib chops, about 2 1/2 lbs. (1.1 kg)	6	6
Medium parsnips, halved lengthwise	3	3
Medium pears (with peel), cored and quartered	3	3
Medium baking potatoes (with peel), cut into 1/4 inch (6 mm) thick slices	3	3
Salt	1/2 tsp.	2 mL

Combine first 7 ingredients in shallow dish.

Add chops. Turn until coated. Cover. Chill overnight.

Transfer to ungreased large roasting pan. Add remaining 4 ingredients. Bake, uncovered, in 400°F (205°C) oven for about 1 1/4 hours, stirring once or twice, until chops are tender and browned. Remove and discard garlic. Serves 6.

1 serving: 305 Calories; 11.9 g Total Fat (6.5 g Mono, 1.2 g Poly, 3.1 g Sat); 42 mg Cholesterol; 31 g Carbohydrate; 5 g Fibre; 21 g Protein; 206 mg Sodium

Pictured on page 144.

Fiery Sweet Pork Chops

The refreshing Cucumber Sauce, that can be served on the side, will cool your palate. It makes the perfect complement to these hot chops. Adjust the amount of vindaloo curry paste to suit your taste.

Mango chutney	1/4 cup	60 mL
Vindaloo curry paste (see Note)	2 tsp.	10 mL
Salt	1/4 tsp.	1 mL
Pepper	1/4 tsp.	1 mL
Cooking oil	1 tbsp.	15 mL
Bone-in pork loin rib end chops (3/4 inch, 2 cm, thick), about 1 3/4 lbs. (790 g)	4	4

CUCUMBER SAUCE

Plain yogurt	2/3 cup	150 mL
Finely chopped peeled and seeded English cucumber	1/3 cup	75 mL
Finely chopped and seeded tomato	1/3 cup	75 mL
Finely chopped red onion	3 tbsp.	50 mL
Lemon juice	2 tsp.	10 mL
Salt, sprinkle		
Pepper, sprinkle		

Combine first 4 ingredients in small bowl.

Heat cooking oil in large frying pan on medium. Add chops. Cook for 5 minutes. Turn. Brush with 1/2 of chutney mixture. Cook for 5 minutes. Turn. Brush with remaining chutney mixture. Cook for 1 minute. Turn. Cook for about 1 minute until chops are tender.

Cucumber Sauce: Combine all 7 ingredients in medium bowl. Makes 1 1/3 cups (325 mL) sauce. Serve with chops. Serves 4.

1 serving: 263 Calories; 14.4 g Total Fat (6.5 g Mono, 2.4 g Poly, 4.2 g Sat); 56 mg Cholesterol; 12 g Carbohydrate; 1 g Fibre; 20 g Protein; 300 mg Sodium

Note: Available in Asian section of grocery stores. Vindaloo curry paste is very hot with a distinct, slightly sour taste.

Sweet And Sour Pork Chops

These lean, tender chops are simmered in a rich,
brown sweet and sour sauce. Delicious!

All-purpose flour	1 1/2 tbsp.	25 mL
Paprika	1 1/2 tsp.	7 mL
Lemon pepper	3/4 tsp.	4 mL
Garlic powder	1/2 tsp.	2 mL
Cayenne pepper	1/4 tsp.	1 mL
Bone-in fast-fry pork loin chops (about 8)	2 lbs.	900 g
Cooking oil	2 tbsp.	30 mL
Can of crushed pineapple (with juice)	14 oz.	398 mL
Brown sugar, packed	1/2 cup	125 mL
Apple cider vinegar	1/3 cup	75 mL
Water	1/4 cup	60 mL
Sweet (or regular) chili sauce	2 tbsp.	30 mL
Indonesian sweet (or thick) soy sauce	1 tbsp.	15 mL
Salt	1/2 tsp.	2 mL
Slivered green pepper	1/2 cup	125 mL
Slivered red pepper	1/2 cup	125 mL
Medium roma (plum) tomato, diced	1	1

Combine first 5 ingredients in small bowl.

Rub both sides of chops with flour mixture.

Heat cooking oil in large frying pan or Dutch oven on medium-high. Add chops. Cook for about 2 minutes per side until browned. Remove to plate. Drain and discard drippings, leaving any brown bits in pan.

Add next 7 ingredients. Bring to a boil, stirring and scraping up any brown bits from bottom of pan. Add chops. Spoon pineapple mixture over chops. Reduce heat to medium-low. Cover. Simmer for 30 minutes.

Add green and red peppers and tomato. Stir. Cover. Cook for about 5 minutes until peppers are tender-crisp. Serves 4 to 6.

1 serving: 588 Calories; 18.8 g Total Fat (9.3 g Mono, 3.5 g Poly, 4.5 g Sat); 142 mg Cholesterol; 54 g Carbohydrate; 2 g Fibre; 51 g Protein; 641 mg Sodium

Chops, Steaks & Ribs

Simple Chops And Gravy

*Add some mashed potatoes and cooked vegetables
to these chops for a comforting, homey meal.*

Bone-in fast-fry pork loin chops (1/2 inch, 12 mm, thick), about 1 1/2 lbs. (680 g)	6	6
Seasoned salt	1/4 tsp.	1 mL
Garlic and herb no-salt seasoning (such as Mrs. Dash)	1/4 tsp.	1 mL
Pepper	1/8 tsp.	0.5 mL
Cooking oil	2 tbsp.	30 mL
All-purpose flour	3 tbsp.	50 mL
Water	1 1/2 cups	375 mL
Beef (or vegetable) bouillon powder	1 tsp.	5 mL
Pepper, sprinkle		

Sprinkle both sides of chops with seasoned salt, no-salt seasoning and first amount of pepper.

Heat cooking oil in large frying pan on medium-high. Add chops. Cook for about 2 minutes per side until browned. Remove to plate.

Sprinkle flour into same frying pan. Cook on medium-low for about 1 minute, stirring constantly, until combined with drippings and browned. Slowly add water, stirring with whisk, until boiling and thickened. Add bouillon powder and second amount of pepper. Stir. Add chops. Cover. Simmer for about 10 minutes until chops are tender and desired doneness is reached. Serves 4.

1 serving: 262 Calories; 13.6 g Total Fat (7.1 g Mono, 2.8 g Poly, 2.8 g Sat); 69 mg Cholesterol; 5 g Carbohydrate; trace Fibre; 28 g Protein; 139 mg Sodium

 When storing chops, steaks and burger patties in the refrigerator or freezer, place a double layer of waxed paper between them to make them easier to separate later on.

Marsala Pork

These tender, thin portions of pork are served in a smooth, creamy sauce. The subtle hint of wine complements the overall flavour of the dish. For a special occasion, serve with steamed broccoli and buttered noodles.

Hard margarine (or butter)	1 tbsp.	15 mL
Cooking oil	1 tbsp.	15 mL
Fresh small white mushrooms, quartered	2 cups	500 mL
Hard margarine (or butter)	1 tbsp.	15 mL
Cooking oil	2 tsp.	10 mL
Boneless pork leg steaks (1/4 inch, 6 mm, thick), about 1 1/2 lbs. (680 g)	4	4
Whipping cream	1 cup	250 mL
Marsala wine	1/3 cup	75 mL
Worcestershire sauce	2 tsp.	10 mL
Salt	1/4 tsp.	1 mL
Pepper, just a pinch		
Finely chopped fresh parsley (or 2 1/4 tsp., 11 mL, flakes)	3 tbsp.	50 mL

Heat first amounts of margarine and cooking oil in large frying pan on medium. Add mushrooms. Cook for about 5 minutes, stirring occasionally, until lightly browned. Remove from pan.

Heat second amounts of margarine and cooking oil in same frying pan on medium. Add steaks. Cook for about 2 minutes per side until just tender. Remove from pan.

Put next 5 ingredients into same frying pan. Heat and stir on medium for about 5 minutes until slightly thickened. Reduce heat to medium-low. Add mushrooms and steaks. Turn until coated. Heat for 1 to 2 minutes until heated through.

Add parsley. Stir. Serves 4.

1 serving: 470 Calories; 36.1 g Total Fat (12.9 g Mono, 3 g Poly, 18.1 g Sat); 191 mg Cholesterol; 4 g Carbohydrate; 1 g Fibre; 30 g Protein; 304 mg Sodium

Pork Steak And Prunes

The addition of dried prunes adds interest to this dish. The sauce is sweet
with a fruity undertone. Spoon it over brown rice for a delicious treat.

Hard margarine (or butter)	1 tbsp.	15 mL
Boneless pork shoulder butt steaks	6	6
(3/8 inch, 1 cm, thick), about		
1 1/2 lbs. (680 g)		
Salt, sprinkle		
Pepper, sprinkle		
Hard margarine (or butter)	1 tbsp.	15 mL
Sliced onion	1 cup	250 mL
Apple juice	3/4 cup	175 mL
Apple cider vinegar	1 tbsp.	15 mL
Granulated sugar	1 tbsp.	15 mL
Worcestershire sauce	1 1/2 tsp.	7 mL
Dried pitted prunes, halved	18	18

Melt first amount of margarine in large frying pan on medium-high. Add
steaks. Cook for about 2 minutes per side, sprinkling with salt and pepper,
until browned. Place in shallow dish or 9 x 13 inch (22 x 33 cm) pan.

Melt second amount of margarine in same frying pan on medium-high.
Add onion. Cook for 1 to 2 minutes, stirring and scraping up any brown
bits from bottom of pan, until starting to brown. Divide and spoon
onto steaks.

Combine next 4 ingredients in small bowl. Carefully pour over onion.

Scatter prunes over steak mixture. Cover tightly with foil. Bake in 350°F
(175°C) oven for about 1 1/4 hours until steaks are tender. Arrange steaks,
onion and prunes on warm platter. Drain liquid into large frying pan. Bring
to a boil. Boil for about 5 minutes until liquid is reduced to about 1/2 cup
(125 mL). Pour over steaks. Serves 6.

1 serving: 299 Calories; 11.6 g Total Fat (4.6 g Mono, 1 g Poly, 5 g Sat); 84 mg Cholesterol;
24 g Carbohydrate; 2 g Fibre; 25 g Protein; 136 mg Sodium

Cajun Steaks

These perfectly grilled steaks are topped with a deliciously seasoned lime butter.

Boneless pork loin steaks (1 inch, 2.5 cm, thick), about 1 1/2 lbs. (680 g)	4	4
Cajun seasoning	1 tbsp.	15 mL
LIME BUTTER		
Cooking oil	1 tbsp.	15 mL
Finely chopped red pepper	1/3 cup	75 mL
Garlic cloves, minced (or 1/2 tsp., 2 mL, powder)	2	2
Butter (or hard margarine), softened	1/4 cup	60 mL
Finely chopped fresh parsley (or 1 1/2 tsp., 7 mL, flakes)	2 tbsp.	30 mL
Finely grated lime zest	1 tsp.	5 mL

Rub both sides of steaks with seasoning. Place in shallow dish. Cover. Chill for at least 3 hours or overnight.

Lime Butter: Heat cooking oil in frying pan on medium. Add red pepper and garlic. Cook for about 5 minutes, stirring occasionally, until red pepper is softened. Turn into small bowl. Cool.

Add butter, parsley and lime zest. Stir until combined. Place on centre of sheet of waxed paper. Roll into 4 inch (10 cm) long log. Chill for 1 to 3 hours until firm. Makes about 1/2 cup (125 mL) butter. Preheat electric grill for 5 minutes or gas barbecue to medium. Cook steaks on greased grill for 6 to 7 minutes per side until tender. Remove and discard waxed paper from butter mixture. Cut log into eight 1/2 inch (12 mm) slices. Just before serving, top each steak with 2 slices. Serves 4.

1 serving: 336 Calories; 22.8 g Total Fat (8.3 g Mono, 2.2 g Poly, 10.9 g Sat); 132 mg Cholesterol; 3 g Carbohydrate; 1 g Fibre; 29 g Protein; 233 mg Sodium

Lemon Garlic Steaks

A rich, lemony sauce coats these tender steaks.

Cooking oil	1 tbsp.	15 mL
Boneless pork loin steaks (1 inch, 2.5 cm, thick), about 1 1/2 lbs. (680 g)	4	4

(continued on next page)

Hard margarine (or butter)	1 tbsp.	15 mL
Garlic cloves, minced (or 1/2 tsp., 2 mL, powder)	2	2
Lemon juice	1/4 cup	60 mL
Chopped fresh dill (or 1 1/2 tsp., 7 mL, dill weed)	2 tbsp.	30 mL
Worcestershire sauce	1 tsp.	5 mL
Salt	1/4 tsp.	1 mL
Pepper	1/4 tsp.	1 mL
Whipping cream	1 cup	250 mL

Heat cooking oil in large frying pan on medium. Add steaks. Cook for about 4 minutes per side until tender. Remove from pan. Keep warm.

Melt margarine in same frying pan on medium-low. Add garlic. Heat and stir for about 1 minute until fragrant.

Add next 5 ingredients. Heat and stir until combined.

Add whipping cream. Bring to a boil. Boil gently for about 5 minutes until thickened. Add steaks. Turn until coated. Serves 4.

1 serving: 416 Calories; 31.1 g Total Fat (10.8 g Mono, 2.2 g Poly, 16.2 g Sat); 169 mg Cholesterol; 4 g Carbohydrate; trace Fibre; 30 g Protein; 269 mg Sodium

Easiest Ribs

The tender meat falls right off of these ribs. This is an effortless slow cooker recipe. For best results, use well-trimmed ribs.

Fancy (mild) molasses	1/3 cup	75 mL
Low-sodium soy sauce	1/3 cup	75 mL
Garlic cloves, minced (or 3/4 tsp., 4 mL, powder)	3	3
Dried crushed chilies	1/4 tsp.	1 mL
Sweet and sour cut pork ribs, trimmed of fat and cut into 1-bone portions	3 1/2 – 4 lbs.	1.6 – 1.8 kg

Combine first 4 ingredients in 3 1/2 quart (3.5 L) slow cooker.

Add ribs. Stir until coated. Cook on Low for 7 to 8 hours or on High for 3 1/2 to 4 hours, stirring once or twice, until very tender. Serves 6.

1 serving: 419 Calories; 19.3 g Total Fat (8.7 g Mono, 2.1 g Poly, 6.7 g Sat); 149 mg Cholesterol; 13 g Carbohydrate; trace Fibre; 46 g Protein; 569 mg Sodium

Finger Lickin' Ribs

Your family will devour these large, oven-baked ribs! Their tangy tomato-based coating is complemented by a wonderful blend of spices.

Country-style ribs (about 12), cut into 1-bone portions	3 – 3 1/2 lbs.	1.4 – 1.6 kg
Pepper, generous sprinkle		
Water	1 cup	250 mL
FINGER LICKIN' SAUCE		
Can of crushed tomatoes	14 oz.	398 mL
Water	1 cup	250 mL
Brown sugar, packed	1/4 cup	60 mL
Liquid honey	1/4 cup	60 mL
Juice and grated peel of large lemon	1	1
Green onions, chopped	3	3
Garlic cloves, halved (or 3/4 tsp., 4 mL, powder)	3	3
Tomato paste	2 tbsp.	30 mL
Beef bouillon concentrate	2 tsp.	10 mL
Curry paste	2 tsp.	10 mL
Worcestershire sauce	2 tsp.	10 mL
Chili powder	2 tsp.	10 mL
Paprika	2 tsp.	10 mL

Sprinkle ribs generously with pepper. Place in ungreased large roasting pan. Add water. Cover. Bake in 325°F (160°C) oven for about 1 1/2 hours until almost tender. Drain liquid. Keep warm.

Finger Lickin' Sauce: Process all 13 ingredients in blender until smooth. Pour into medium saucepan. Bring to a boil. Reduce heat to medium-low. Simmer, uncovered, for 10 minutes to blend flavours. Pour over ribs. Turn until coated. Bake, uncovered, in 325°F (160°C) oven for about 1 hour, stirring several times, until ribs are reddish-brown and very tender. Serves 8.

1 serving: 370 Calories; 14.9 g Total Fat (6.6 g Mono, 1.7 g Poly, 5.1 g Sat); 112 mg Cholesterol; 25 g Carbohydrate; 2 g Fibre; 35 g Protein; 228 mg Sodium

Sweet And Sour Ribs

These tasty ribs are coated with a tangy but sweet sauce.
The flavour is absolutely delicious!

Cooking oil	1 tbsp.	15 mL
Sweet and sour cut pork ribs, trimmed of fat and cut into 1-bone portions	3 lbs.	1.4 kg
Tomato juice	1 cup	250 mL
Brown sugar, packed	2/3 cup	150 mL
White vinegar	1/2 cup	125 mL
Soy sauce	1 tbsp.	15 mL
Water	1 tbsp.	15 mL
Cornstarch	1 tbsp.	15 mL

Heat 1 1/2 tsp. (7 mL) cooking oil in large frying pan on medium-high. Add 1/2 of ribs. Cook for 8 to 10 minutes, stirring frequently, until browned. Transfer to greased small roasting pan. Repeat with remaining cooking oil and ribs.

Measure next 4 ingredients into small saucepan. Bring to a boil.

Stir water into cornstarch in small bowl. Stir into tomato juice mixture until thickened. Pour over ribs. Cover. Bake in 350°F (175°C) oven for 45 to 60 minutes until ribs are very tender. Serves 4.

1 serving: 734 Calories; 32.4 g Total Fat (15.1 g Mono, 4.2 g Poly, 10.2 g Sat); 224 mg Cholesterol; 40 g Carbohydrate; 1 g Fibre; 68 g Protein; 551 mg Sodium

Variation: Omit browning ribs in cooking oil. Instead put ribs into large pot or Dutch oven. Cover with water. Bring to a boil. Boil for 1 hour. Drain. Transfer to greased small roasting pan. Proceed with recipe but only bake for about 30 minutes until very tender.

 When serving sticky finger foods, such as ribs, prepare individual finger bowls for your guests. Fill small bowls with very warm water. Place a thin lemon or lime slice on top. Pair each bowl with a paper napkin.

Pork With The Works

Tender pork and roasted potatoes are a great combination. The delicious gravy has a sweet citrus undertone. This recipe makes a filling evening meal.

Grainy mustard	2 tbsp.	30 mL
Finely chopped fresh sage (or 3/4 tsp., 4 mL, dried)	1 tbsp.	15 mL
Cooking oil	2 tsp.	10 mL
Garlic cloves, minced (or 1/2 tsp., 2 mL, powder)	2	2
Salt	1/2 tsp.	2 mL
Pepper	1/4 tsp.	1 mL
Boneless pork loin rib end roast	4 1/2 lbs.	2 kg
Cooking oil	1 tbsp.	15 mL
Medium potatoes, peeled and quartered	6	6
GRAVY		
All-purpose flour	3 tbsp.	50 mL
Prepared chicken broth	1 cup	250 mL
Orange juice	1 cup	250 mL
Red currant jelly	1/3 cup	75 mL
Brandy (or 1/4 tsp., 1 mL, flavouring)	1 tbsp.	15 mL
Hard margarine (or butter)	1 tbsp.	15 mL

Combine first 6 ingredients in small bowl.

Rub roast with mustard mixture, reserving 1 tbsp. (15 mL). Put roast into large roasting pan.

Stir reserved mustard mixture and second amount of cooking oil in large bowl. Add potato. Toss until coated. Arrange potato in single layer around roast. Cook, uncovered, in 425°F (220°C) oven for 30 minutes. Turn roast and potato. Cook for about 1 1/4 hours until meat thermometer inserted in centre of roast reads 155°F (68°C) or until desired doneness. Transfer potato to greased baking sheet. Bake, uncovered, in 350°F (175°C) oven for 10 minutes. Remove roast to large serving platter. Cover with foil. Let stand for 10 minutes. Internal temperature should rise to at least 160°F (70°C). Carve into 1/2 inch (12 mm) thick slices.

(continued on next page)

Entrees

Gravy: Drain all but 2 tbsp. (30 mL) juices from roasting pan. Add flour. Cook on medium for 1 to 2 minutes, stirring constantly, until combined and browned.

Add broth, orange juice and jelly. Heat and stir until boiling and thickened.

Add brandy. Heat and stir for 3 to 5 minutes to blend flavours. Reduce heat to low.

Add margarine. Stir until melted. Makes 2 cups (500 mL) gravy. Serve with pork and potato. Makes seventeen 3 oz. (85 g) pork servings.

1 serving: 240 Calories; 9.8 g Total Fat (4.5 g Mono, 1.3 g Poly, 3.2 g Sat); 67 mg Cholesterol; 9 g Carbohydrate; 1 g Fibre; 27 g Protein; 187 mg Sodium

---

Fettuccine Carbonara

A delightful, creamy sauce coats these long, flat noodles. The bacon and the savoury flavour of the Parmesan cheese go very well together. Serve with a green salad and sliced ripe tomatoes.

Package of fettuccine	8 3/4 oz.	250 g
Boiling water	8 cups	2 L
Salt	1 tsp.	5 mL
Bacon slices, chopped	8	8
Whipping cream	1 cup	250 mL
Large eggs, fork-beaten	3	3
Finely grated fresh Parmesan cheese	1 cup	250 mL
Salt	1/4 tsp.	1 mL
Pepper, sprinkle		

Cook fettuccine in boiling water and first amount of salt in large uncovered pot or Dutch oven for about 10 minutes until tender but firm. Drain well. Return to pot.

Cook bacon in medium frying pan on medium-high for about 5 minutes until crisp. Drain.

Add whipping cream. Heat and stir for 2 to 3 minutes until hot. Add to fettuccine. Stir.

Add egg and cheese. Stir until combined.

Add second amount of salt and pepper. Stir. Makes 4 cups (1 L).

1 cup (250 mL): 683 Calories; 36.7 g Total Fat (11.8 g Mono, 2.1 g Poly, 20.3 g Sat); 260 mg Cholesterol; 51 g Carbohydrate; 2 g Fibre; 36 g Protein; 2005 mg Sodium

Vegetable Pork Loaf

This attractive meatloaf contains a complex blend of vegetables and seasonings. It slices easily and would be great in a sandwich.

Fresh whole wheat bread slices, torn	3	3
Lean ground pork	1 1/2 lbs.	680 g
Green onions, cut into 4 pieces each	4	4
Large egg	1	1
Medium carrot, cut into 4 pieces	1	1
Red pepper, seeded and cut into 4 pieces	1/2	1/2
Sun-dried (or roasted and dried) tomatoes, softened in boiling water for 10 minutes and finely diced	1/3 cup	75 mL
Garlic cloves, halved (or 1/2 tsp., 2 mL, powder), optional	2	2
Worcestershire sauce	2 tsp.	10 mL
Seasoned salt	1 1/2 tsp.	7 mL
Hot pepper sauce	1/2 tsp.	2 mL
Dried thyme	1/4 tsp.	1 mL
Dried marjoram	1/4 tsp.	1 mL
Pepper	1/4 tsp.	1 mL

Process bread in blender until consistency of fine crumbs. Transfer to large bowl.

Add ground pork. Mix.

Put remaining 12 ingredients into blender. Pulse with on/off motion until chopped. Process for 10 to 15 seconds until very finely chopped. Add to pork mixture. Mix well. Shape into 10 x 3 x 2 inch (25 x 7.5 x 5 cm) loaf. Place in foil-lined greased 9 x 13 inch (22 x 33 cm) pan. Bake, uncovered, in 350°F (175°C) oven for 1 to 1 1/4 hours until meat thermometer inserted in centre reads 170°F (77°C). Drain and discard drippings at halftime if necessary. Cuts into 12 slices. Serves 6.

1 serving: 309 Calories; 18.4 g Total Fat (8 g Mono, 1.8 g Poly, 6.6 g Sat); 88 mg Cholesterol; 11 g Carbohydrate; 2 g Fibre; 25 g Protein; 478 mg Sodium

Paré Pointer

When you're really hungry, you eat a hot dog with relish.

Glazed Meatloaf

Bits of onion and parsley are visible inside this moist, flavourful meatloaf. Serve hot with mashed potatoes and steamed vegetables or cold in sandwiches.

Lean ground pork	1/2 lb.	225 g
Lean ground beef	1/2 lb.	225 g
Fine dry bread crumbs	1 cup	250 mL
Finely chopped onion	1 cup	250 mL
Grated carrot	1/2 cup	125 mL
Finely chopped celery	1/3 cup	75 mL
Chopped fresh parsley (or 2 1/4 tsp., 11 mL, flakes)	3 tbsp.	50 mL
Ketchup	2 tbsp.	30 mL
Worcestershire sauce	1 tbsp.	15 mL
Large egg, fork-beaten	1	1
GLAZE		
Ketchup	1/3 cup	75 mL
Brown sugar, packed	1/4 cup	60 mL
Water	1/4 cup	60 mL
Worcestershire sauce	3 tbsp.	50 mL
Malt vinegar	2 tbsp.	30 mL
Lemon juice	2 tbsp.	30 mL

Combine first 10 ingredients in large bowl. Shape into 10 inch (25 cm) long roll. Place on foil-lined baking sheet with sides. Bake in 350°F (175°C) oven for 30 minutes.

Glaze: Combine all 6 ingredients in small bowl. Makes 1 1/4 cups (300 mL) glaze. Pour 1/2 over shaped pork mixture. Bake for about 30 minutes, brushing occasionally with remaining glaze, until firm, browned and glazed. Cuts into twenty 1/2 inch (12 mm) slices.

1 slice: 99 Calories; 3.8 g Total Fat (1.7 g Mono, 0.3 g Poly, 1.4 g Sat); 22 mg Cholesterol; 11 g Carbohydrate; 1 g Fibre; 6 g Protein; 168 mg Sodium

Pictured on page 54.

Ham Steaks With Cherries

A pretty pink, translucent sauce with bits of cherry covers these juicy Black Forest ham steaks. The sauce carries a sweet hint of orange and cloves. Have your butcher cut steaks with a small circumference from a Black Forest ham. That way, an entire steak may be served to each guest.

Black Forest ham slices (1/4 inch, 6 mm, thick), about 1 1/2 lbs. (680 g)	6	6
Ginger ale	1 cup	250 mL
Maraschino cherry syrup	1/4 cup	60 mL
White vinegar	2 tbsp.	30 mL
Cornstarch	1 1/2 tbsp.	25 mL
Dry mustard	1 tsp.	5 mL
Finely grated orange peel	1 tsp.	5 mL
Maraschino cherries, quartered	10	10
Ground cloves, just a pinch		
Ground cinnamon, just a pinch		

Arrange ham slices in single layer on foil-lined baking sheet with sides.

Combine remaining 9 ingredients in small saucepan. Heat and stir on medium for about 8 minutes until boiling and thickened. Pour over ham. Bake, uncovered, in 350°F (175°C) oven for about 30 minutes until ham is heated through and glazed. Serves 6.

1 serving: 247 Calories; 18.6 g Total Fat (8.8 g Mono, 2 g Poly, 6.6 g Sat); 46 mg Cholesterol; 11 g Carbohydrate; trace Fibre; 9 g Protein; 713 mg Sodium

1. Tomato Pork Curry, page 68
2. Apricot Sauce, page 148
3. Fruited Calzones, page 50
4. Apricot Pork Loin Roast, page 110

Props Courtesy Of: Danesco Inc.
Stokes

Entrees

Creamy Baked Ham Slice

Make sure you use a thick ham steak so the delicious, creamy sauce can cook down without drying out the meat. This will be a big hit with your family!

Hard margarine (or butter)	2 tsp.	10 mL
All-purpose flour	2 tsp.	10 mL
Prepared mustard	2 tsp.	10 mL
Boneless ham slice (1 inch, 2.5 cm, thick), trimmed of fat	1 lb.	454 g
Evaporated milk (not skim)	1 cup	250 mL
Brown sugar, packed	2 tbsp.	30 mL

Line 9 x 9 inch (22 x 22 cm) pan with foil. Coat foil with margarine.

Combine flour and mustard in small bowl.

Rub both sides of ham with flour mixture. Place ham in pan.

Pour evaporated milk over ham. Sprinkle with brown sugar. Bake, uncovered, in 375°F (190°C) oven for about 1 hour until liquid is reduced by about 1/3. Stir, incorporating any solids that have formed during baking. Cut ham into 4 pieces. Serves 4.

1 serving: 254 Calories; 9.6 g Total Fat (3.9 g Mono, 0.7 g Poly, 4 g Sat); 69 mg Cholesterol; 17 g Carbohydrate; trace Fibre; 24 g Protein; 1389 mg Sodium

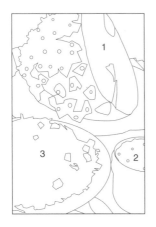

1. Barbecue Glazed Ham, page 135
2. Tomato Pear Relish, page 145
3. Ham Slaw, page 41

Props Courtesy Of: Island Pottery Inc.

Ham And Sea Pizza

This unique pizza incorporates a variety of textures, colours,
flavours and shapes—a very tasty combination!

Cooking oil	2 tsp.	10 mL
Chopped onion	1/2 cup	125 mL
Pizza sauce	1/2 cup	125 mL
Prebaked pizza crust (or flatbread), 12 inch (30 cm) diameter	1	1
Grated medium Cheddar cheese	1/3 cup	75 mL
Grated part-skim mozzarella cheese	1/3 cup	75 mL
Diced cooked ham	3/4 cup	175 mL
Cooked salad shrimp	1/2 cup	125 mL
Chopped green pepper	1/2 cup	125 mL
Chopped fresh white mushrooms	1/3 cup	75 mL
Chopped red pepper	1/4 cup	60 mL
Grated medium Cheddar cheese	1/4 cup	60 mL
Grated part-skim mozzarella cheese	1/4 cup	60 mL

Heat cooking oil in medium frying pan on medium. Add onion. Cook for about 5 minutes, stirring often, until softened.

Add pizza sauce. Stir.

Place crust on ungreased pizza pan. Spread onion mixture evenly over crust.

Combine first amounts of Cheddar cheese and mozzarella cheese in small bowl. Scatter over onion mixture.

Scatter next 5 ingredients over cheese.

Combine second amounts of Cheddar cheese and mozzarella cheese in same bowl. Scatter over ham mixture. Bake on bottom rack in 425°F (220°C) oven for 12 to 15 minutes until cheese is melted and crust is golden. Cuts into 8 wedges.

1 wedge: 322 Calories; 13.3 g Total Fat (4.8 g Mono, 1.2 g Poly, 6.5 g Sat); 64 mg Cholesterol; 30 g Carbohydrate; 2 g Fibre; 20 g Protein; 906 mg Sodium

Bacon Mushroom Pizza

This thick, cheesy pizza is easy to make and it tastes fantastic!
The smoky bacon and the savoury seasonings complement
the earthy flavour of the mushrooms.

Thick bacon slices	12	12
Prebaked pizza crust (or flatbread), 12 inch (30 cm) diameter	1	1
Pizza sauce	1/3 cup	75 mL
Grated Edam (or mozzarella) cheese	3/4 cup	175 mL
Sliced fresh mushrooms	2 cups	500 mL
Dried thyme, sprinkle		
Pepper, sprinkle		
Thinly sliced provolone (or mozzarella) cheese	6 1/3 oz.	180 g

Cook bacon in frying pan on medium for 10 to 15 minutes until browned. Remove to paper towels to drain. Drain and discard all but 1 tbsp. (15 mL) drippings from pan. Cut bacon into 1/2 inch (12 mm) pieces.

Place crust on ungreased pizza pan. Spread with pizza sauce.

Sprinkle with Edam cheese. Scatter bacon over cheese.

Heat reserved drippings in same frying pan on medium. Add mushrooms. Cook for about 5 minutes, stirring often, until liquid is evaporated. Scatter over bacon.

Sprinkle with thyme and pepper.

Top with provolone cheese. Bake on bottom rack in 425°F (220°C) oven for about 10 minutes until cheese is melted. Cuts into 8 wedges.

1 wedge: 303 Calories; 12 g Total Fat (4.4 g Mono, 0.7 g Poly, 6.1 g Sat); 42 mg Cholesterol; 27 g Carbohydrate; 1 g Fibre; 21 g Protein; 1195 mg Sodium

Paré Pointer

A giraffe with a sore neck seems pretty bad unless you
think of a centipede with corns.

Italian Sausage With Rice

This attractive dish originated in Northern Italy. Use hot sausage for a little extra zip in the meat sauce. Serve it over pasta instead of rice if desired.

SAUSAGE MEAT SAUCE

Italian sausages (about 1 lb., 454 g), casings removed	5	5
Chopped onion	1 cup	250 mL
Sliced fresh white mushrooms	1 cup	250 mL
Can of diced tomatoes (with juice)	28 oz.	796 mL
Granulated sugar	1 tsp.	5 mL
Salt	1/4 tsp.	1 mL
Pepper	1/8 tsp.	0.5 mL

FLAVOURED RICE

Prepared chicken broth	4 cups	1 L
Long grain white rice	2 cups	500 mL
Water	1/4 cup	60 mL
Hard margarine (or butter)	2 tbsp.	30 mL
Finely grated fresh Parmesan cheese, for garnish	1/4 cup	60 mL
Chopped fresh parsley, for garnish		

Sausage Meat Sauce: Scramble-fry sausage and onion in large frying pan on medium-high for about 8 minutes, stirring constantly, until sausage is browned. Drain.

Add mushrooms. Reduce heat to medium. Cook for about 3 minutes, stirring constantly, until browned.

Add next 4 ingredients. Stir. Bring to a boil. Reduce heat to medium-low. Simmer, uncovered, for 20 minutes. Makes 4 cups (1 L) sauce. Keep warm.

Flavoured Rice: Combine first 4 ingredients in medium saucepan. Bring to a boil. Reduce heat to medium-low. Cover. Simmer for about 15 minutes until rice is tender and liquid is absorbed. Fluff with fork. Makes 6 cups (1.5 L) rice. Arrange on large serving platter or individual plates. Spoon sauce over rice.

Sprinkle with cheese and parsley. Serves 4.

1 serving: 960 Calories; 45.7 g Total Fat (19.3 g Mono, 5.4 g Poly, 18.2 g Sat); 92 mg Cholesterol; 102 g Carbohydrate; 3 g Fibre; 33 g Protein; 2347 mg Sodium

Pictured on page 71.

Meatballs In Tomato Sauce

A rich, creamy tomato sauce surrounds these tasty meatballs.

Lean ground pork	3/4 lb.	340 g
Lean ground beef	1/2 lb.	225 g
Fine dry bread crumbs	1/2 cup	125 mL
Pecans, toasted (see Tip, page 105) and finely chopped	1/2 cup	125 mL
Basil pesto	1/3 cup	75 mL
Large egg, fork-beaten	1	1
Olive (or cooking) oil	1 tbsp.	15 mL
Olive (or cooking) oil	1 tbsp.	15 mL
Chopped onion	1 1/2 cups	375 mL
Garlic cloves, minced (or 1/2 tsp., 2 mL, powder)	2	2
Can of diced tomatoes (with juice)	28 oz.	796 mL
Balsamic vinegar	1 tbsp.	15 mL
Brown sugar, packed	2 tsp.	10 mL
Salt	1/4 tsp.	1 mL
Pepper, sprinkle		
Whipping cream	1 cup	250 mL

Combine first 6 ingredients in large bowl. Shape into balls using 2 tbsp. (30 mL) mixture for each. Chill for 30 minutes. Makes about 22 meatballs.

Heat first amount of olive oil in large frying pan on medium. Add meatballs. Cook for about 15 minutes, turning occasionally, until browned and no longer pink inside. Remove from pan.

Wipe frying pan with paper towels. Heat second amount of olive oil in same frying pan on medium. Add onion and garlic. Cook for 5 to 10 minutes, stirring often, until softened.

Add next 5 ingredients. Stir. Bring to a boil. Reduce heat. Simmer for about 5 minutes, stirring occasionally, until thickened.

Add whipping cream. Stir. Add meatballs. Heat and stir for about 5 minutes until hot and bubbling. Serves 6.

1 serving: 635 Calories; 49.3 g Total Fat (24.6 g Mono, 4.9 g Poly, 16.4 g Sat); 130 mg Cholesterol; 26 g Carbohydrate; 4 g Fibre; 24 g Protein; 528 mg Sodium

Pork Nachos

These spectacular nachos are bursting with fresh, southwestern flavours.

Cooking oil	1 tbsp.	15 mL
Finely chopped onion	1 cup	250 mL
Finely chopped red pepper	1 cup	250 mL
Garlic cloves, minced (or 1 tsp., 5 mL, powder)	4	4
Taco seasoning mix, stir before measuring	2 tbsp.	30 mL
Salt	1/4 tsp.	1 mL
Lean ground pork	3/4 lb.	340 g
Boneless, skinless chicken breast halves (4 oz., 113 g, each), finely chopped	2	2
Salsa	1/2 cup	125 mL
Bag of white corn chips	11 oz.	310 g
Grated medium Cheddar cheese	1 cup	250 mL
Finely chopped seeded tomato	1 cup	250 mL
Finely chopped avocado	1 cup	250 mL
Finely chopped red onion	1/3 cup	75 mL
Lemon juice	1 tbsp.	15 mL
Sliced pickled jalapeño pepper, chopped (optional)	1 tbsp.	15 mL
Garlic clove, minced (or 1/4 tsp., 1 mL, powder)	1	1
Salt, sprinkle		
Pepper, sprinkle		
Sour cream	1/2 cup	125 mL
Chopped fresh chives	2 tbsp.	30 mL

Heat cooking oil in large frying pan on medium. Add onion, red pepper and first amount of garlic. Cook for 5 to 10 minutes, stirring often, until onion is softened.

Add seasoning mix. Heat and stir for about 1 minute until fragrant.

Add first amount of salt, ground pork and chicken. Scramble-fry on medium-high for 5 to 10 minutes until browned. Remove from heat.

(continued on next page)

Entrees

Add salsa. Stir until combined.

Place corn chips in ovenproof shallow dish. Top with pork mixture. Sprinkle with cheese. Broil on top rack in oven for 2 to 3 minutes until cheese is melted.

Combine next 8 ingredients in medium bowl. Spoon over cheese.

Spoon sour cream over tomato mixture. Sprinkle with chives. Serves 6.

1 serving: 799 Calories; 52.9 g Total Fat (19.3 g Mono, 11.6 g Poly, 17.9 g Sat); 105 mg Cholesterol; 47 g Carbohydrate; 7 g Fibre; 38 g Protein; 851 mg Sodium

---

Mediterranean Pie

This lovely golden pie tastes of sun-dried tomatoes and prosciutto ham. Use cooked chopped bacon in place of the ham if you prefer. Serve with a fresh garden salad to complete the meal.

All-purpose flour	1/3 cup	75 mL
Milk	1 1/2 cups	375 mL
Large eggs	3	3
Sliced prosciutto (or deli) ham, coarsely chopped	4 oz.	113 g
Finely grated fresh Parmesan cheese	2/3 cup	150 mL
Sun-dried tomatoes in oil, drained and chopped	1/2 cup	125 mL
Large green olives (about 9), pitted and chopped	1/3 cup	75 mL
Chopped fresh parsley (or 2 1/4 tsp., 11 mL, flakes)	3 tbsp.	50 mL

Combine flour, milk and eggs in medium bowl until smooth.

Add remaining 5 ingredients. Mix well. Pour into greased flan dish or 9 inch (22 cm) pie plate. Bake in 325°F (160°C) oven for about 1 hour until wooden pick inserted in centre comes out clean. Cuts into 8 wedges.

1 wedge: 162 Calories; 8.7 g Total Fat (3.6 g Mono, 0.8 g Poly, 3.6 g Sat); 90 mg Cholesterol; 9 g Carbohydrate; 1 g Fibre; 13 g Protein; 634 mg Sodium

Pictured on page 143.

Stove-Top Cutlets

Fresh zucchini is a delightful addition to this creamy, tomato-based dish.
The delicate hint of wine rounds out the flavour of the meat.

All-purpose flour	2 tbsp.	30 mL
Paprika	1 tsp.	5 mL
Salt	1/2 tsp.	2 mL
Lemon pepper	1/2 tsp.	2 mL
Pork cutlets (about 1 lb., 454 g)	4	4
Cooking oil	1 tbsp.	15 mL
Dry white (or alcohol-free) wine	1/4 cup	60 mL
Sliced small zucchini (with peel)	2 cups	500 mL
Can of Italian-style stewed tomatoes (with juice), mashed	14 oz.	398 mL
Sliced green onion	2/3 cup	150 mL
Garlic clove, minced (or 1/4 tsp., 1 mL, powder), optional	1	1
Ground rosemary	1/8 tsp.	0.5 mL
Half-and-half cream	1/2 cup	125 mL
All-purpose flour	2 tbsp.	30 mL
Finely grated fresh Parmesan cheese (optional)	2 tbsp.	30 mL

Combine first 4 ingredients in shallow dish.

Dredge cutlets in flour mixture.

Heat cooking oil in large frying pan on medium-high. Add cutlets. Cook for about 4 minutes per side until browned.

Add wine. Bring to a boil, scraping up any brown bits from bottom of pan.

Add next 5 ingredients. Stir. Reduce heat to medium-low. Cover. Simmer for 30 to 40 minutes until cutlets are tender. Remove cutlets to large serving platter. Keep warm.

Mix cream and second amount of flour in small bowl until smooth. Add to tomato mixture. Heat and stir until boiling and thickened. Pour over cutlets.

Sprinkle with cheese. Serves 4.

1 serving: 298 Calories; 10.9 g Total Fat (4.7 g Mono, 1.8 g Poly, 3.6 g Sat); 101 mg Cholesterol; 20 g Carbohydrate; 3 g Fibre; 29 g Protein; 557 mg Sodium

Jellied Pork Slices

Tender pork and savoury seasonings are suspended in a clear, firm jelly.
This cold entree goes well with mustard and rye bread and can
be served up for lunch or for a light supper.

Pork hocks (3 1/2 – 4 lbs., 1.6 – 1.8 kg)	4	4
Water, to cover		
Whole black peppercorns	10	10
Garlic cloves, halved (not powder)	5	5
Bay leaves	2	2
Celery ribs, cut into 4 pieces each	2	2
Large onion, cut into 4 wedges	1	1
Salt	4 tsp.	20 mL
Finely chopped pimiento (optional)	1 tbsp.	15 mL
Finely chopped fresh chives (or 3/4 tsp., 4 mL, dried)	1 tbsp.	15 mL

Put hocks into large pot or Dutch oven. Add water. Bring to a boil. Cook, uncovered, for 1 minute. Drain. Wash hocks in clean water. Return to pot. Cover with fresh water. Bring to a boil.

Add next 6 ingredients. Stir. Reduce heat to medium-low. Cover. Simmer for about 4 hours until meat is falling off bones and very tender. Strain stock through sieve and reserve. Remove meat from hocks. Discard bones and any other solids. Cut meat into bite-size pieces. Arrange in single layer in ungreased 9 x 9 inch (22 x 22 cm) glass dish.

Sprinkle with pimiento and chives. Cover with plastic wrap. Chill. Cool stock in deep bowl until thickened. Skim fat off top. Carefully pour 2 1/2 to 3 cups (625 to 750 mL) over meat until covered. Shake dish slightly to fill empty spaces. Chill, uncovered, until set. Scrape off and discard any remaining fat. Cuts into 18 pieces. Serves 6.

1 serving: 193 Calories; 12.1 g Total Fat (5.6 g Mono, 1.4 g Poly, 4.1 g Sat); 67 mg Cholesterol; 6 g Carbohydrate; 1 g Fibre; 15 g Protein; 1624 mg Sodium

Pork Schnitzel

These tender slices of pork are coated in a crisp cornflake
crumb coating. The meat is juicy and well seasoned.

All-purpose flour	1/4 cup	60 mL
Seasoned salt	2 tsp.	10 mL
Paprika	1 tsp.	5 mL
Garlic powder (optional)	1/4 tsp.	1 mL
Pepper	1/4 tsp.	1 mL
Cayenne pepper	1/8 tsp.	0.5 mL
Large egg	1	1
Milk	1/4 cup	60 mL
Cornflake (or fine dry bread) crumbs	1 cup	250 mL
Boneless pork inside leg roast, cut into 1/4 inch (6 mm) slices (see Note)	1 1/2 lbs.	680 g
Cooking oil	2 tbsp.	30 mL
Chopped fresh parsley, for garnish		
Lemon wedges, for garnish		

Combine first 6 ingredients in small bowl. Spread onto sheet of waxed paper.

Beat egg and milk with fork in shallow dish or pie plate.

Spread cornflake crumbs on separate sheet of waxed paper.

Pound pork slices with rolling pin or flat mallet between 2 sheets of waxed paper until about 1/8 inch (3 mm) thick. Cut in half if very large. Press each slice of pork into flour mixture. Dip into egg mixture. Press each slice into cornflake crumbs until coated.

Heat 1 tbsp. (15 mL) cooking oil in large frying pan on medium. Add 1/2 of pork. Cook for 1 1/2 to 2 minutes per side until cooked and golden brown. Transfer to warm platter. Wipe frying pan with paper towel. Repeat with remaining cooking oil and pork.

Garnish with parsley and lemon. Serves 6.

1 serving: 281 Calories; 9.5 g Total Fat (4.8 g Mono, 2 g Poly, 2 g Sat); 122 mg Cholesterol; 20 g Carbohydrate; 1 g Fibre; 27 g Protein; 583 mg Sodium

Note: To slice the leg roast more easily, cut it partially frozen. Or ask the meat cutter to slice it.

Roasted Pork Dinner

Serve this flavourful dish with a salad and Chunky Applesauce, page 148.
Use less garlic if preferred.

Garlic cloves, minced (or 1 1/2 tsp., 7 mL, powder)	6	6
Olive (or cooking) oil	2 tbsp.	30 mL
Seasoned salt	2 tsp.	10 mL
Coarsely ground pepper (or 1/2 tsp., 2 mL, pepper)	1 tsp.	5 mL
Paprika	1 tsp.	5 mL
Parsley flakes	1 tsp.	5 mL
Dried thyme	1/2 tsp.	2 mL
Boneless pork shoulder butt roast, rolled and tied	2 – 2 1/2 lbs.	900 g – 1.1 kg
Baby carrots (about 3 cups, 750 mL)	1 lb.	454 g
Sweet potatoes (or yams), about 1 lb. (454 g), peeled, quartered lengthwise and cut into 1 1/2 inch (3.8 cm) chunks	2	2
Unpeeled medium red potatoes (about 1 1/2 lbs., 680 g), quartered lengthwise and cut into 1 1/2 inch (3.8 cm) chunks	3	3
Olive (or cooking) oil	2 tbsp.	30 mL
Parsley flakes	2 tsp.	10 mL
Seasoned salt	1 tsp.	5 mL
Pepper, sprinkle		

Combine first 7 ingredients in small bowl until consistency of thick paste.

Rub paste over roast until coated. Place on greased wire rack in large greased roasting pan. Cover. Cook in 350°F (175°C) oven for 45 minutes.

Arrange carrots, sweet potato and red potato around roast.

Combine remaining 4 ingredients in separate small bowl. Drizzle over vegetables. Stir. Cover. Cook for 45 to 60 minutes until meat thermometer inserted into thickest part of roast reads 155°F (68°C) or until desired doneness. Remove roast. Cover with foil. Let stand for 10 minutes. Internal temperature should rise to at least 160°F (70°C). Stir vegetables in roasting pan. Increase heat to 450°F (230°C). Cook vegetables, uncovered, for 10 to 15 minutes until tender and starting to brown. Serve with sliced roast. Makes 8 to 10 three oz. (85 g) meat servings.

1 serving: 336 Calories; 14.6 g Total Fat (8.4 g Mono, 1.5 g Poly, 3.5 g Sat); 71 mg Cholesterol; 25 g Carbohydrate; 5 g Fibre; 26 g Protein; 540 mg Sodium

Pictured on page 107.

Roasts

Polenta-Stuffed Loin

Your guests will be impressed by this striking presentation and wonderful flavour.

POLENTA STUFFING

Olive (or cooking) oil	2 tsp.	10 mL
Diced red pepper	1/4 cup	60 mL
Sliced green onion	1/4 cup	60 mL
Garlic cloves, minced (or 1/2 tsp., 2 mL, powder)	2	2
Prepared chicken broth	1 cup	250 mL
Parsley flakes	2 tsp.	10 mL
Dried crushed chilies	1/4 tsp.	1 mL
Pepper, sprinkle		
Yellow cornmeal	1/2 cup	125 mL
Boneless pork loin roast	3 1/2 – 4 lbs.	1.6 – 1.8 kg
Yellow cornmeal	3 tbsp.	50 mL
Seasoned salt	2 tsp.	10 mL
Paprika	2 tsp.	10 mL
Garlic powder	1 tsp.	5 mL
Coarsely ground pepper (or 1/2 tsp., 2 mL, pepper)	1 tsp.	5 mL

Polenta Stuffing: Heat olive oil in large non-stick frying pan on medium. Add red pepper, onion and garlic. Cook for 2 to 3 minutes, stirring often, until softened.

Add next 4 ingredients. Bring to a boil. Reduce heat to medium-low.

Slowly stir in first amount of cornmeal. Heat and stir until mixture sticks together and no liquid remains. Turn out onto sheet of parchment paper. Let stand until cool enough to handle. Shape into two 5 inch (12.5 cm) long logs. Freeze for about 2 hours until firm.

Cut string from roast. Cut deep, wide slits into roast in an X pattern from centre of each end using sharp knife. Insert 1 frozen polenta log into each end to meet in middle of roast. Trim off and discard any excess polenta as necessary.

Combine remaining 5 ingredients in small bowl. Spread evenly across sheet of waxed paper. Roll roast in cornmeal mixture until coated. Place on greased wire rack in roasting pan or 9 x 13 inch (22 x 33 cm) pan. Cook, uncovered, in 325°F (160°C) oven for 1 3/4 to 2 hours until meat thermometer inserted into thickest part of roast (not stuffing) reads 155°F (68°C) or until desired doneness. Cover with foil. Let stand for 10 minutes. Internal temperature should rise to at least 160°F (70°C). Cut into 1/2 to 3/4 inch (1.2 to 2 cm) thick slices. Makes twelve 3 oz. (85 g) servings.

(continued on next page)

1 serving: 221 Calories; 6 g Total Fat (2.8 g Mono, 0.7 g Poly, 1.9 g Sat); 92 mg Cholesterol; 9 g Carbohydrate; 1 g Fibre; 32 g Protein; 158 mg Sodium

Pictured on page 71.

Spiced Roast

This roast is coated in a dark, well-seasoned rub that is absorbed nicely into the meat. Serve with buttered couscous or rice.

Pork leg butt half roast, trimmed of fat	4 1/2 – 5 1/2 lbs.	2 – 2.5 kg
Garlic cloves, quartered lengthwise	2	2
White vinegar	3 tbsp.	50 mL
Brown sugar, packed	1 tbsp.	15 mL
Dry mustard	2 tsp.	10 mL
Finely grated peeled gingerroot	1 tsp.	5 mL
Ground cumin	1 tsp.	5 mL
Ground coriander	1 tsp.	5 mL
Chili paste (sambal oelek)	1/2 – 1 tsp.	2 – 5 mL
Ground cardamom	1/2 tsp.	2 mL
Ground cinnamon	1/2 tsp.	2 mL
Salt	1/2 tsp.	2 mL
Ground cloves	1/4 tsp.	1 mL
Pepper	1/4 tsp.	1 mL

Make 8 shallow diagonal cuts across roast. Push 1 piece of garlic into each cut.

Combine remaining 12 ingredients in small bowl. Rub over roast. Place roast in shallow dish. Cover. Chill for at least 8 hours or overnight. Transfer to greased wire rack on baking sheet. Cook, uncovered, in 350°F (175°C) oven for about 2 1/2 hours until meat thermometer inserted into thickest part of roast reads 155°F (68°C) or until desired doneness. Cover with foil. Let stand for 10 minutes. Internal temperature should rise to at least 160°F (70°C). Cut into 1/4 inch (6 mm) thick slices. Makes 18 to 22 three oz. (85 g) servings.

1 serving: 161 Calories; 6 g Total Fat (2.7 g Mono, 0.7 g Poly, 2 g Sat); 68 mg Cholesterol; 2 g Carbohydrate; trace Fibre; 24 g Protein; 131 mg Sodium

Crown Pork Roast

This attractive, elegant crown roast will be the centrepiece of the evening. An excellent item to serve for a special occasion, but remember to order it ahead.

Crown pork roast	8 lbs.	3.6 kg
Cooking oil	1 tbsp.	15 mL
Salt	1/2 tsp.	2 mL
HAZELNUT AND APRICOT STUFFING		
Bacon slices, chopped	4	4
Finely chopped onion	3/4 cup	175 mL
Coarse fresh bread crumbs	1 1/2 cups	375 mL
Chopped dried apricots	2/3 cup	150 mL
Hazelnuts (filberts), toasted (see Tip, page 105) and chopped	2/3 cup	150 mL
Orange juice	1/4 cup	60 mL
Chopped fresh thyme leaves (or 1 1/2 tsp., 7 mL, dried)	2 tbsp.	30 mL
Large egg, fork-beaten	1	1
Tart medium cooking apple (such as Granny Smith), grated	1	1
Finely grated orange zest	1 tsp.	5 mL
APPLE ORANGE GRAVY		
All-purpose flour	1/4 cup	60 mL
Orange juice	1 cup	250 mL
Prepared chicken broth	1 cup	250 mL
Applesauce	1/2 cup	125 mL
Brandy (or 3/4 tsp., 4 mL, flavouring)	3 tbsp.	50 mL
Grainy mustard	2 tbsp.	30 mL
Salt	1/4 tsp.	1 mL
Pepper	1/4 tsp.	1 mL

Place roast, bones pointing up, on greased wire rack in roasting pan. Rub with cooking oil. Sprinkle with salt. Fill cavity with large ball of foil. Cover bone tips with small pieces of foil. Cook, uncovered, in 325°F (160°C) oven for 1 hour.

(continued on next page)

Hazelnut And Apricot Stuffing: Cook bacon and onion in frying pan on medium for about 10 minutes, stirring occasionally, until bacon is starting to brown. Transfer to large bowl.

Add next 8 ingredients. Mix well. Makes 4 cups (1 L) stuffing. Remove roast from oven. Carefully remove foil from cavity. Spoon stuffing into cavity. Press down lightly. Cook for 1 1/2 to 2 hours, covering stuffing loosely with foil for last 30 minutes, until meat thermometer inserted into thickest part of roast (not stuffing) reads 155°F (68°C) or until desired doneness. Cover with foil. Let stand for 10 minutes. Internal temperature should rise to at least 160°F (70°C). Remove foil from bones before serving.

Apple Orange Gravy: Drain all but 1/4 cup (60 mL) drippings from roasting pan. Add flour. Cook on medium for about 1 minute, stirring constantly, until combined and browned.

Add remaining 7 ingredients. Stir. Bring to a boil. Boil for about 5 minutes, stirring until thickened. Strain through sieve. Discard any solids. Makes 2 cups (500 mL) gravy. Serve with roast and stuffing. Makes 14 one-bone portions.

1 serving: 616 Calories; 29.2 g Total Fat (14.4 g Mono, 3.5 g Poly, 8.7 g Sat); 187 mg Cholesterol; 23 g Carbohydrate; 2 g Fibre; 61 g Protein; 571 mg Sodium

Pictured on front cover.

 tip   *To toast nuts and seeds, place in single layer in ungreased shallow pan. Bake in 350°F (175°C) oven for 5 to 10 minutes, stirring or shaking often, until desired doneness.*

Orange-Glazed Roast

This roast is brown and glossy on the outside and tender and juicy on the inside. The mild citrus flavour enhances the succulence of the meat.

Orange marmalade	1/2 cup	125 mL
Orange juice	1/2 cup	125 mL
Grainy mustard	1/4 cup	60 mL
Chili sauce	2 tbsp.	30 mL
Salt	1/4 tsp.	1 mL
Pork loin rib end roast	2 3/4 lbs.	1.25 kg

Combine first 5 ingredients in small bowl.

Place roast on greased wire rack in roasting pan. Cook, uncovered, in 350°F (175°C) oven for 1 hour. Brush with marmalade mixture. Cook for 1 to 1 1/4 hours, brushing several times with remaining marmalade mixture, until meat thermometer inserted into thickest part of roast reads 155°F (68°C) or until desired doneness. Cover with foil. Let stand for 10 minutes. Internal temperature should rise to at least 160°F (70°C). Cut between bones into individual chops. Serves 6.

1 serving: 443 Calories; 18.7 g Total Fat (8.5 g Mono, 2 g Poly, 6.4 g Sat); 138 mg Cholesterol; 22 g Carbohydrate; 1 g Fibre; 46 g Protein; 371 mg Sodium

1. Mushroom Tarragon Sauce, page 142
2. Roasted Pork Dinner, page 101

Props Courtesy Of: Pfaltzgraff Canada

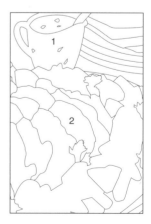

Crusty Ham Roast

This sweet, juicy ham is coated in an attractive golden crust.

PASTE		
Brown sugar, packed	2/3 cup	150 mL
All-purpose flour	1/3 cup	75 mL
Prepared mustard	2 tbsp.	30 mL
White vinegar	1 tbsp.	15 mL
Ground cloves	1/4 tsp.	1 mL
Cooked boneless ham	8 lbs.	3.6 kg

Paste: Combine first 5 ingredients in small bowl. Makes 1/2 cup (125 mL) paste.

Blot ham dry with paper towel. Spread paste onto bottom of ham. Place in roasting pan. Coat top and sides with remaining paste. Cook, uncovered, in 350°F (175°C) oven for about 1 1/2 hours until heated through and outside is browned. Makes thirty-two 3 oz. (85 g) servings.

1 serving: 162 Calories; 6.2 g Total Fat (2.9 g Mono, 0.6 g Poly, 2 g Sat); 60 mg Cholesterol; 6 g Carbohydrate; trace Fibre; 19 g Protein; 1265 mg Sodium

1. Pork Wonton Soup, page 32, with Sweet Cold Pork Slices, page 15
2. Lemon Grass Pork Bowl, page 120
3. Honey Ginger Pork, page 116

Props Courtesy Of: Island Pottery Inc.
Pier 1 Imports

Apricot Pork Loin Roast

This elegant roast is perfect for entertaining. Your guests will admire its elegant presentation. Leftovers are great in a sandwich or served with a salad.

STUFFING

Bag of fresh spinach, stems removed	10 oz.	285 g
Boiling water		
White bread cubes (about 8 slices, crusts removed)	4 cups	1 L
Finely chopped onion	1 cup	250 mL
Chopped dried apricots	1 cup	250 mL
Hard margarine (or butter), melted	1/3 cup	75 mL
Chopped fresh parsley (or 1 tbsp., 15 mL, flakes)	1/4 cup	60 mL
Apricot jam	3 tbsp.	50 mL
Garlic cloves, minced (or 1/2 tsp., 2 mL, powder)	2	2
Salt	1/4 tsp.	1 mL
Boneless pork loin roast	4 1/2–5 1/2 lbs.	2–2.5 kg
Grainy mustard	1/4 cup	60 mL
Apricot jam	3 tbsp.	50 mL
Grainy mustard	2 tbsp.	30 mL

Stuffing: Cook spinach in small amount of boiling water in medium saucepan until just wilted. Drain. Cool slightly. Squeeze dry.

Combine next 8 ingredients in large bowl.

Cut roast in half lengthwise. Place roast halves, cut sides up, on work surface. Spread cut sides with first amount of mustard. Spread 1/2 of bread mixture over 1 half. Cover with spinach. Layer with remaining bread mixture. Top with other half of roast, mustard-side down. Tie with butcher's string at about 1 1/4 inch (3 cm) intervals. Place on greased wire rack in roasting pan. Cook, uncovered, in 325°F (160°C) oven for 1 hour.

Combine second amounts of jam and mustard in small bowl. Spread over roast in even layer. Cook for about 1 hour until meat thermometer inserted into thickest part of roast (not stuffing) reads 155°F (68°C) or until desired doneness. Cover with foil. Let stand for 10 minutes. Internal temperature should rise to at least 160°F (70°C). Cut into 1/2 inch (12 mm) thick slices. Makes 18 to 22 three oz. (85 g) servings.

(continued on next page)

1 serving: 253 Calories; 7.9 g Total Fat (2.9 g Mono, 0.8 g Poly, 3.5 g Sat); 87 mg Cholesterol; 18 g Carbohydrate; 2 g Fibre; 27 g Protein; 268 mg Sodium

Pictured on page 89.

Walnut-Stuffed Tenderloin

The moist stuffing has a delicate blue cheese flavour with a sweet hint of apple and a nutty undertone. This is excellent served hot or cold.

Olive (or cooking) oil	1 tbsp.	15 mL
Finely chopped onion	1 cup	250 mL
Garlic cloves, minced (or 1/2 tsp., 2 mL, powder)	2	2
Finely chopped tart cooking apple (such as Granny Smith)	3/4 cup	175 mL
Day-old bread crumbs	1/2 cup	125 mL
Walnuts, toasted (see Tip, page 105) and chopped	1/4 cup	60 mL
Crumbled blue cheese	2 – 3 tbsp.	30 – 50 mL
Large egg, fork-beaten	1	1
Chopped fresh thyme leaves (or 1/2 tsp., 2 mL, dried)	2 tsp.	10 mL
Pork tenderloins (about 1 1/2 lbs., 680 g, total)	2	2
Salt, sprinkle		
Coarsely ground pepper, sprinkle		

Heat olive oil in frying pan on medium. Add onion and garlic. Cook for 5 to 10 minutes, stirring often, until softened. Transfer to medium bowl.

Add next 6 ingredients. Mix well.

Cut tenderloins almost in half lengthwise, but not quite through, to other side. Press open to flatten. Pound with mallet or rolling pin to even thickness. Divide and spread onion mixture on cut sides of tenderloins. Roll up from long side, jelly roll-style. Tie with butcher's string or secure with metal skewers. Place on greased wire racks on baking sheets. Sprinkle with salt and pepper. Cook, uncovered, in 375°F (190°C) oven for about 50 minutes until meat thermometer inserted into thickest part of tenderloins (not stuffing) reads 155°F (68°C) or until desired doneness. Cover with foil. Let stand for 10 minutes. Internal temperature should rise to at least 160°F (70°C). Cut into 1 inch (2.5 cm) thick slices. Makes six 3 oz. (85 g) servings.

1 serving: 301 Calories; 10.8 g Total Fat (4.6 g Mono, 2.8 g Poly, 2.6 g Sat); 101 mg Cholesterol; 18 g Carbohydrate; 2 g Fibre; 32 g Protein; 232 mg Sodium

Roasts

Slow Cooker Baked Ham

This very tender ham is drizzled with a tangy citrus-flavoured sauce. Cooking your ham in the slow cooker frees up your oven for the preparation of side dishes.

Cooked boneless ham (not frozen, see Note)	3 lbs.	1.4 kg
CITRUS SAUCE		
Brown sugar, packed	1/2 cup	125 mL
Frozen concentrated orange juice, thawed	2 tbsp.	30 mL
Grainy (or prepared) mustard	1 tbsp.	15 mL
Prepared horseradish	2 tsp.	10 mL
Water	2/3 cup	150 mL
Lemon juice	3 tbsp.	50 mL
Cornstarch	2 tbsp.	30 mL

Put ham into 3 1/2 quart (3.5 L) slow cooker.

Citrus Sauce: Combine first 4 ingredients in small dish. Pour over ham. Cover. Cook on Low for 4 to 5 hours or on High for 2 to 2 1/2 hours. Remove ham from slow cooker. Cut in half lengthwise. Place halves, cut sides down, on work surface. Carve, across grain on diagonal, into 1/4 inch (6 mm) thick slices. Arrange on serving platter. Keep warm.

Pour juices from slow cooker into small saucepan. Add water.

Stir lemon juice into cornstarch in small dish until smooth. Add slowly to ham juices. Heat and stir on medium for 3 to 4 minutes until boiling and thickened. Makes about 1 cup (250 mL) sauce. Drizzle over ham slices. Makes twelve 3 oz. (85 g) servings.

1 serving: 195 Calories; 6.4 g Total Fat (3 g Mono, 0.6 g Poly, 2.1 g Sat); 62 mg Cholesterol; 14 g Carbohydrate; trace Fibre; 20 g Protein; 1320 mg Sodium

Note: Frozen ham creates too much moisture in the slow cooker, resulting in boiling instead of cooking.

Diced Pork Skillet Supper

This is a creative, tasty way to use up leftover pork chops and rice. This delicious stir-fry contains a pleasant mix of fresh vegetables, pork, rice and egg.

Cooking oil	1 tbsp.	15 mL
Sliced fresh mushrooms	1 cup	250 mL
Diced onion	1/2 cup	125 mL
Diced celery	1/2 cup	125 mL
Diced red pepper	1/2 cup	125 mL
Cooking oil	1 tbsp.	15 mL
Large eggs	2	2
Leftover cooked pork chops or steaks, meat cut from bones and diced 1/2 inch (12 mm), about 8 oz. (225 g)	1 – 2 cups	250 – 500 mL
Frozen peas	2/3 cup	150 mL
Cold cooked rice	3 cups	750 mL
Salt	1/2 tsp.	2 mL
Pepper	1/4 tsp.	1 mL
Soy sauce	3 tbsp.	50 mL

Sliced green onion, for garnish

Heat wok or large frying pan on medium. Add first amount of cooking oil. Add next 4 ingredients. Stir-fry for about 3 minutes until vegetables are softened. Transfer to bowl.

Add second amount of cooking oil to hot wok. Add eggs. Break yolks. Cook, without stirring, until starting to set. Turn over. Cut egg with straight edge of pancake lifter in 1 direction. Cut across in opposite direction to make small diced pieces.

Add pork and peas. Stir-fry for 1 to 2 minutes until peas are thawed.

Add rice, salt and pepper. Stir-fry for about 5 minutes until rice is separated and heated through. Add mushroom mixture.

Add soy sauce slowly, stirring until mixture is combined and evenly coloured.

Sprinkle with onion. Makes 7 cups (1.75 L). Serves 4.

1 serving: 431 Calories; 12.7 g Total Fat (6.4 g Mono, 2.9 g Poly, 2.3 g Sat); 122 mg Cholesterol; 57 g Carbohydrate; 3 g Fibre; 21 g Protein; 1031 mg Sodium

Pork And Shrimp Noodles

Red peppers and pink shrimp add colour and texture to this noodle dish.

Fresh fine egg noodles (about 1/3 lb., 150 g)	4 cups	1 L
Boiling water	2 cups	500 mL
Salt	1 1/2 tsp.	7 mL
Cooking oil	1 1/2 tsp.	7 mL
Soy sauce	2 tbsp.	30 mL
Cornstarch	2 tsp.	10 mL
Hoisin sauce	2 tbsp.	30 mL
Liquid honey	2 tbsp.	30 mL
Dry sherry	2 tbsp.	30 mL
Water	2 tbsp.	30 mL
Chili paste (sambal oelek)	1/2 – 1 tsp.	2 – 5 mL
Cooking oil	2 tsp.	10 mL
Raw medium shrimp, peeled and deveined	12 oz.	340 g
Cooking oil	1 tbsp.	15 mL
Medium onion, halved and cut into 12 wedges	1	1
Chopped red pepper	1 cup	250 mL
Garlic cloves, minced (or 1/2 tsp., 2 mL, powder)	2	2
Finely grated peeled gingerroot	1 tsp.	5 mL
Lean ground pork	3/4 lb.	340 g
Thinly sliced cabbage	2 cups	500 mL

Cook noodles in boiling water and salt in uncovered medium saucepan for 1 minute. Drain. Transfer to large bowl.

Add first amount of cooking oil. Toss. Set aside.

Stir soy sauce into cornstarch in small bowl. Add next 5 ingredients. Stir. Set aside.

Heat wok or large frying pan on medium-high. Add second amount of cooking oil. Add shrimp. Stir-fry for about 2 minutes until starting to turn pink. Transfer to separate small bowl.

Add third amount of cooking oil to hot wok. Add next 4 ingredients. Stir-fry for about 1 minute until fragrant.

Add ground pork. Scramble-fry for about 5 minutes until pork is browned and no pink remains. Stir cornstarch mixture. Add to pork mixture. Stir-fry for about 1 minute until boiling and thickened.

(continued on next page)

Stir-Fries

Add noodles and cabbage. Stir-fry for about 2 minutes until mixture is well combined and cabbage is tender-crisp. Add shrimp. Stir. Makes about 7 cups (1.75 L).

1 cup (250 mL): 333 Calories; 13.5 g Total Fat (6.1 g Mono, 2.6 g Poly, 3.4 g Sat); 119 mg Cholesterol; 29 g Carbohydrate; 2 g Fibre; 23 g Protein; 868 mg Sodium

---

Egg Foo Yong

Each bite of these omelets contains an excellent combination of flavours and textures. They can be served with the complementary sauce or on their own.

Large eggs	6	6
Salt	1/2 tsp.	2 mL
Cooking oil	1 tbsp.	15 mL
Pork tenderloin, trimmed of fat and cut into strips	8 oz.	225 g
Fresh bean sprouts (about 3 cups, 750 mL), chopped once or twice	8 oz.	225 g
Thinly sliced celery	1/3 cup	75 mL
Sliced green onion	1/3 cup	75 mL
Light-coloured (or regular) soy sauce	1 tbsp.	15 mL
Cooking oil	1 tbsp.	15 mL
SAUCE		
Prepared chicken broth	1 cup	250 mL
Oyster sauce	1 tbsp.	15 mL
Cornstarch	1 tbsp.	15 mL
Fancy (mild) molasses	1 tbsp.	15 mL

Beat eggs and salt with fork in large bowl. Set aside.

Heat large non-stick frying pan on medium-high. Add first amount of cooking oil. Add pork. Stir-fry for 1 minute. Add bean sprouts, celery and onion. Stir-fry for 2 to 3 minutes until slightly softened.

Add soy sauce. Cover. Cook for 3 minutes. Remove cover. Add to egg mixture. Stir.

Add 1/2 tsp. (2 mL) of second amount of cooking oil to hot frying pan. Add about 1/3 cup (75 mL) egg mixture for each omelet. Cook on medium for about 2 minutes, turning at halftime, until set and lightly browned. Remove to serving platter. Keep warm. Repeat with remaining cooking oil and egg mixture.

Sauce: Combine all 4 ingredients in small saucepan. Heat and stir on medium for 5 to 10 minutes until boiling and thickened. Makes about 1 cup (250 mL) sauce. Serve over Egg Foo Yong. Serves 4.

1 serving: 277 Calories; 16.1 g Total Fat (8.1 g Mono, 3.4 g Poly, 3.4 g Sat); 312 mg Cholesterol; 7 g Carbohydrate; trace Fibre; 24 g Protein; 807 mg Sodium

Honey Ginger Pork

These golden, bite-size pieces of pork are enhanced by the orange carrot and green onion slices. A sweet ginger flavour dominates the dish.

Large eggs	2	2
Garlic cloves, minced (or 1/2 tsp., 2 mL, powder)	2	2
Finely grated peeled gingerroot	2 tsp.	10 mL
Sesame (or cooking) oil	1 tsp.	5 mL
Salt	1/2 tsp.	2 mL
Pork tenderloin, trimmed of fat	1 lb.	454 g
Pancake mix	1/2 cup	125 mL
Cornstarch	1/4 cup	60 mL
Water	1/4 cup	60 mL
Cornstarch	1 1/2 tsp.	7 mL
Cooking oil, for deep-frying		
Sesame (or cooking) oil	2 tsp.	10 mL
Green onions, sliced (see Tip, page 27)	2	2
Medium carrot, cut lengthwise and thinly sliced	1	1
Finely grated peeled gingerroot	1 tbsp.	15 mL
Liquid honey	1/3 cup	75 mL
Oyster sauce	1 1/2 tbsp.	25 mL
Dried crushed chilies	1/4 – 1/2 tsp.	1 – 2 mL

Put first 5 ingredients into medium bowl. Beat with fork.

Cut tenderloin in half lengthwise. Cut crosswise into 1/4 inch (6 mm) thick slices. Add to egg mixture. Stir well.

Combine pancake mix and first amount of cornstarch in small cup. Add to pork mixture. Stir until pork is coated.

Stir water into second amount of cornstarch in small bowl.

Deep-fry pork, in 2 batches, in hot (375°F, 190°C) cooking oil for 3 to 4 minutes, stirring and keeping pork pieces separate, until golden brown. Remove to paper towels to drain. Arrange on serving platter. Keep warm.

Heat wok or large frying pan on medium-high. Add second amount of sesame oil. Add onion, carrot and second amount of ginger. Stir-fry for about 2 minutes until onion is softened.

(continued on next page)

Add honey, oyster sauce and chilies. Stir-fry for 1 minute. Stir cornstarch mixture. Stir into vegetable mixture until boiling and thickened. Pour over pork. Serves 4 to 6.

1 serving: 549 Calories; 20.9 g Total Fat (10.5 g Mono, 5.7 g Poly, 3.2 g Sat); 160 mg Cholesterol; 58 g Carbohydrate; 2 g Fibre; 34 g Protein; 580 mg Sodium

Pictured on page 108.

Ginger Pork

If you love the taste of ginger, this dish is for you! The slight heat from the cayenne pepper will linger in your mouth. Serve with rice noodles.

Sesame (or cooking) oil	2 tbsp.	30 mL
Cornstarch	1/4 cup	60 mL
Boneless pork loin, cut julienne	1 lb.	454 g
Cayenne pepper	1/4 tsp.	1 mL
Cooking oil	1 tbsp.	15 mL
Medium carrots, cut julienne	2	2
Finely chopped peeled gingerroot	2 tbsp.	30 mL
Medium onion, cut lengthwise into slivers	1	1
Cooking oil	1 tbsp.	15 mL
Fish sauce	3 tbsp.	50 mL
Indonesian sweet (or thick) soy sauce	2 tbsp.	30 mL

Chopped fresh cilantro (or fresh parsley),
    for garnish
Sliced green onion, for garnish

Stir sesame oil into cornstarch in medium bowl. Add pork and cayenne pepper. Stir until pork is coated. Let stand for 15 minutes.

Heat wok or large frying pan on medium-high. Add first amount of cooking oil. Add carrot, ginger and onion. Stir-fry for about 5 minutes until golden. Transfer to bowl.

Add second amount of cooking oil to hot wok. Add pork mixture. Stir-fry for about 3 minutes, keeping pork pieces separate, until browned and no longer pink inside. Add carrot mixture. Stir.

Add fish sauce and soy sauce. Stir-fry for about 1 minute until pork is coated.

Sprinkle with cilantro and green onion. Makes 4 cups (1 L). Serves 4.

1 serving: 340 Calories; 18.1 g Total Fat (8.7 g Mono, 5.4 g Poly, 2.9 g Sat); 78 mg Cholesterol; 16 g Carbohydrate; 2 g Fibre; 27 g Protein; 1668 mg Sodium

Mongolian Pork

This dish presents well and it tastes great! The subtle flavour
of the Chinese five-spice powder complements the other fresh ingredients.

Soy sauce	1/3 cup	75 mL
Cornstarch	1 1/2 tbsp.	25 mL
Boneless pork loin, cut into 1/8 inch (3 mm) thick strips	1 1/2 lbs.	680 g
Garlic cloves, minced (or 1/2 tsp., 2 mL, powder)	2	2
Large egg, fork-beaten	1	1
Black bean sauce	2 tbsp.	30 mL
Granulated sugar	1 tbsp.	15 mL
Chinese five-spice powder	1 tsp.	5 mL
Sesame oil	1/2 tsp.	2 mL
Peanut (or cooking) oil	1 1/2 tbsp.	25 mL
Peanut (or cooking) oil	1 tbsp.	15 mL
Medium onions, sliced into thin wedges	2	2
Prepared chicken broth	1/2 cup	125 mL
Green onion, thinly sliced (see Tip, page 27)	1	1

Stir soy sauce into cornstarch in large bowl. Add next 7 ingredients. Stir. Cover. Chill for 1 1/2 to 3 hours.

Heat wok or large frying pan on medium-high. Add first amount of peanut oil. Stir-fry pork mixture, in batches, for about 3 minutes until pork is browned and almost cooked. Transfer to bowl.

Add second amount of peanut oil to hot wok. Add onion. Stir-fry for about 3 minutes until softened.

Add broth. Bring to a boil. Stir pork mixture. Stir into onion mixture until sauce is thickened and pork is tender.

Sprinkle with green onion. Serves 4.

1 serving: 392 Calories; 17 g Total Fat (7.6 g Mono, 4.1 g Poly, 4 g Sat); 183 mg Cholesterol; 18 g Carbohydrate; 1 g Fibre; 40 g Protein; 1389 mg Sodium

Cabbage Stir-Fry

This pale cabbage dish is interspersed with bright red peppers.
The tender-crisp veggies are sweet with a very mild heat. A winner!

Soy sauce	1 tbsp.	15 mL
Cornstarch	1 tbsp.	15 mL
Hoisin sauce	3 tbsp.	50 mL
Water	2 tbsp.	30 mL
Sweet (or regular) chili sauce	2 tbsp.	30 mL
Mirin (rice wine)	2 tbsp.	30 mL
Chili paste (sambal oelek)	1 tsp.	5 mL
Cooking oil	2 tsp.	10 mL
Lean ground pork	3/4 lb.	340 g
Sliced brown (or white) mushrooms	2 cups	500 mL
Finely chopped red pepper	1 cup	250 mL
Large onion, cut into thin wedges	1	1
Garlic cloves, minced (or 1/2 tsp., 2 mL, powder)	2	2
Finely grated peeled gingerroot	1 tsp.	5 mL
Finely shredded cabbage	4 cups	1 L
Slivered almonds, toasted (see Tip, page 105)	1/2 cup	125 mL

Stir soy sauce into cornstarch in small bowl. Add next 5 ingredients. Stir. Set aside.

Heat wok or large frying pan on medium-high. Add cooking oil. Add ground pork. Scramble-fry for 5 to 7 minutes until browned and no longer pink. Transfer to bowl.

Add next 5 ingredients to hot wok. Stir-fry for about 2 minutes until fragrant.

Add pork and cabbage. Stir-fry for 2 to 3 minutes until cabbage is starting to soften. Stir cornstarch mixture. Stir into pork mixture for 3 to 4 minutes until mixture is well combined and sauce is thickened.

Add almonds. Stir. Makes 6 cups (1.5 L). Serves 4.

1 serving: 422 Calories; 25.5 g Total Fat (13.2 g Mono, 4.3 g Poly, 5.9 g Sat); 43 mg Cholesterol; 28 g Carbohydrate; 7 g Fibre; 23 g Protein; 447 mg Sodium

Lemon Grass Pork Bowl

Lemon grass, an important ingredient in Thai cuisine, gives this dish a fresh, light flavour. Adjust the amounts of chili sauce and soy sauce to suit your taste.

Soy sauce	1 tbsp.	15 mL
Cornstarch	2 tsp.	10 mL
Fish sauce	3 tbsp.	50 mL
Chili sauce	2 tbsp.	30 mL
Water	2 tbsp.	30 mL
Cooking oil	2 tbsp.	30 mL
Boneless pork shoulder butt roast, cut on diagonal into 1/8 inch (3 mm) thick slices	12 oz.	340 g
Garlic cloves, minced (or 1/2 tsp., 2 mL, powder)	2	2
Stalk of lemon grass, bulb only (root and stalk removed), bruised and finely chopped (or 1 tsp., 5 mL, finely grated lemon peel)	1	1
Dried crushed chilies	1/4 tsp.	1 mL
Medium onion, sliced lengthwise into thin wedges	1	1
Medium carrot, cut julienne	1	1
Package of rice vermicelli	8 oz.	250 g
Boiling water, to cover		
Sliced cucumber (with peel), halved	1/3 cup	75 mL
Fresh mint leaves (not dried)	8	8
Fresh bean sprouts	1/2 cup	125 mL
Shredded iceberg lettuce	1/2 cup	125 mL
Thinly sliced green onion	1/4 cup	60 mL
Chopped roasted peanuts	1/4 cup	60 mL

Stir soy sauce into cornstarch in small bowl. Add fish sauce, chili sauce and water. Stir. Set aside.

Heat wok or large frying pan on medium-high. Add cooking oil. Add next 4 ingredients. Stir-fry for about 30 seconds until pork is turning white.

(continued on next page)

Stir-Fries

Add onion and carrot. Stir-fry for 3 to 4 minutes until carrot is tender-crisp. Stir cornstarch mixture. Stir into pork mixture until boiling and thickened. Remove from heat.

Put vermicelli into large bowl. Add boiling water. Let stand for 2 minutes. Drain.

Divide next 4 ingredients among 4 large individual serving bowls. Cover with vermicelli. Spoon pork mixture over top.

Sprinkle individual servings with green onion and peanuts. Serves 4.

1 serving: 543 Calories; 19.7 g Total Fat (9.9 g Mono, 4.5 g Poly, 3.8 g Sat); 72 mg Cholesterol; 59 g Carbohydrate; 2 g Fibre; 37 g Protein; 2079 mg Sodium

Pictured on page 108.

Plum Ribs

These small ribs are coated in a sticky, sweet sauce that would go very well with steamed jasmine rice. The meat is so tender it is practically falling off the bones!

Sweet and sour cut pork ribs, trimmed of fat and cut into 1-bone portions	3 1/2 lbs.	1.6 kg
Boiling water	4 cups	1 L
Water	1 cup	250 mL
Plum sauce	1/3 cup	75 mL
White vinegar	3 tbsp.	50 mL
Ketchup	3 tbsp.	50 mL
Soy sauce	2 tbsp.	30 mL
Brown sugar, packed	2 tbsp.	30 mL
Garlic cloves, minced (or 1/2 tsp., 2 mL, powder)	2	2
Chili sauce	2 tsp.	10 mL

Heat wok or medium saucepan on medium-high. Add ribs and boiling water. Bring to a boil. Cover. Boil for 30 minutes, stirring occasionally. Drain. Transfer ribs to bowl.

Add remaining 8 ingredients to hot wok. Stir until combined. Bring to a boil. Reduce heat to medium. Add ribs. Cook, uncovered, for about 20 minutes, stirring often, until sauce is very thick and ribs are coated. Makes 8 cups (2 L).

1 cup (250 mL): 360 Calories; 16.7 g Total Fat (7.5 g Mono, 1.9 g Poly, 5.7 g Sat); 128 mg Cholesterol; 11 g Carbohydrate; trace Fibre; 39 g Protein; 489 mg Sodium

Barbecued Tenderloin Slices

This sweet, tangy marinade is so tasty! It is the perfect
complement to these tender, juicy pork slices.

Pork tenderloins (about 1 lb., 454 g, each), trimmed of fat	2	2
MARINADE		
Chili sauce	1/2 cup	125 mL
Ketchup	1/2 cup	125 mL
Apple cider vinegar	1/2 cup	125 mL
Fancy (mild) molasses	1/3 cup	75 mL
Lemon juice	1 tbsp.	15 mL
Worcestershire sauce	2 tsp.	10 mL
Dry mustard	2 tsp.	10 mL

Cut tenderloins almost in half lengthwise, but not quite through, to other side. Press open to flatten. Place in resealable freezer bag.

Marinade: Combine all 7 ingredients in small bowl. Makes about 2 cups (500 mL) marinade. Chill 1/2 of marinade. Pour remaining over tenderloins. Seal. Turn until coated. Marinate in refrigerator for 4 to 6 hours, turning several times. Drain and discard marinade. Preheat gas barbecue to medium. Place tenderloins on greased grill. Close lid. Cook for about 20 minutes, turning several times and brushing with reserved marinade, until meat thermometer inserted in centre reads 155°F (68°C) or until desired doneness. Cover with foil. Let stand for 10 minutes. Internal temperature should rise to at least 160°F (70°C). Cut into 1/2 inch (12 mm) thick slices. Makes eight 3 oz. (85 g) servings.

1 serving: 202 Calories; 3.2 g Total Fat (1.5 g Mono, 0.4 g Poly, 1 g Sat); 67 mg Cholesterol; 15 g Carbohydrate; 1 g Fibre; 28 g Protein; 326 mg Sodium

tip   *When barbecuing or grilling chops and steaks, always use tongs instead of a fork to turn them over. Because a fork pierces the meat, the natural juices will run out, causing the meat to become drier.*

Pesto Pork Burgers

These moist, golden brown patties are flavoured with herbs and sun-dried tomato pesto and topped with fresh salad greens. Delicious!

Lean ground pork	3/4 lb.	340 g
Sun-dried tomato pesto	1/4 cup	60 mL
Fine dry bread crumbs	1/4 cup	60 mL
Chopped fresh parsley (or 2 1/4 tsp., 11 mL, flakes)	3 tbsp.	50 mL
Chopped pitted whole ripe olives	3 tbsp.	50 mL
Large egg, fork-beaten	1	1
Spreadable cream cheese	1/3 cup	75 mL
Dijon mustard	2 tbsp.	30 mL
Chopped fresh thyme leaves (or 1/2 tsp., 2 mL, dried)	2 tsp.	10 mL
Hamburger buns, split and toasted	4	4
Mixed salad greens	1 cup	250 mL

Combine first 6 ingredients in medium bowl. Divide and shape into 4 patties. Preheat electric grill for 5 minutes or gas barbecue to medium-high. Place patties on greased grill. Cook for 5 to 7 minutes per side until no longer pink inside.

Combine cream cheese, mustard and thyme in small bowl. Spread onto cut sides of buns.

Place patty on bottom half of each bun. Top with salad greens and other half of bun. Makes 4 burgers.

1 burger: 450 Calories; 25.2 g Total Fat (10 g Mono, 3 g Poly, 9.6 g Sat); 109 mg Cholesterol; 30 g Carbohydrate; 3 g Fibre; 25 g Protein; 665 mg Sodium

Paré Pointer

Every time the leopard escaped from the zoo, he was always spotted.

Lemon Dill Chops

*A tangy lemon sauce with a hint of dill coats these
tender chops. Your family will love these!*

Mayonnaise	6 tbsp.	100 mL
Dijon mustard	1/4 cup	60 mL
Lemon juice	1/4 cup	60 mL
Dill weed	1 1/2 tsp.	7 mL
Bone-in pork loin chops (about 3/4 inch, 2 cm, thick), trimmed of fat (about 1 1/2 – 1 3/4 lbs., 680 – 790 g)	4	4

Salt, sprinkle
Pepper, sprinkle

Combine first 4 ingredients in small bowl. Pour into large resealable
freezer bag.

Add chops. Seal. Turn until coated. Marinate in refrigerator overnight,
turning several times. Drain marinade into small saucepan. Bring to a boil.
Boil for 5 minutes.

Sprinkle both sides of chops with salt and pepper. Preheat gas barbecue to
medium. Place chops on greased grill. Cook for 7 to 8 minutes per side,
brushing occasionally with marinade, until desired doneness. Serves 4.

*1 serving: 318 Calories; 24.6 g Total Fat (13.2 g Mono, 6.9 g Poly, 3.7 g Sat); 73 mg Cholesterol;
3 g Carbohydrate; 1 g Fibre; 21 g Protein; 344 mg Sodium*

1. Creamy Applesauce, page 147
2. Barbecued Pork Salad, page 44
3. Spiced Pork Chops, page 127

On The Grill

Spiced Pork Chops

These thick, boneless chops have a spicy Cajun feel. The savoury seasonings in the rub would go well with grilled corn, potatoes and a fresh garden salad.

SPICE RUB		
Paprika	1 tsp.	5 mL
Ground oregano	1 tsp.	5 mL
Garlic powder	1 tsp.	5 mL
Chili powder	1/2 tsp.	2 mL
Salt	1/2 tsp.	2 mL
Ground cloves	1/4 tsp.	1 mL
Boneless pork loin chops (about 1 inch, 2.5 cm, thick), about 2 1/2 lbs. (1.1 kg)	6	6

Spice Rub: Combine first 6 ingredients in small bowl. Makes about 1 1/2 tbsp. (25 mL) rub.

Rub on both sides of chops. Place in shallow dish. Cover. Chill for at least 3 hours. Preheat gas barbecue to medium-high. Place chops on greased grill. Cook for about 5 minutes per side until desired doneness. Serves 6.

1 serving: 241 Calories; 6.7 g Total Fat (3 g Mono, 0.8 g Poly, 2.3 g Sat); 127 mg Cholesterol; 1 g Carbohydrate; trace Fibre; 41 g Protein; 280 mg Sodium

Pictured on page 125.

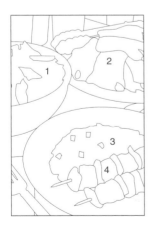

1. Zesty Potato Salad, page 46
2. Barbecue Beer Ribs, page 132
3. Nutty Rice Pilaf, page 140
4. Pepper Pork Skewers, page 136

Props Courtesy Of: Pfaltzgraff Canada

Jerk Pork Chops

The thick coating on these chops is filled with a pleasant variety of spices. A wonderful heat lingers in the aftertaste.

JERK MARINADE

Water	1/2 cup	125 mL
Cooking oil	1/4 cup	60 mL
Large onion, cut into 8 wedges	1	1
Garlic cloves	3	3
Scotch bonnet (or habanero) chili pepper (with seeds for extra heat)	1	1
Piece of peeled gingerroot (about 1 inch, 2.5 cm, long)	1	1
Ground cinnamon	1/2 tsp.	2 mL
Ground allspice	1/2 tsp.	2 mL
Ground oregano	1/8 tsp.	0.5 mL
Bone-in fast-fry pork loin chops (about 1/2 inch, 12 mm, thick), about 8	2 1/4 lbs.	1 kg
Salt	1/2 tsp.	2 mL

Jerk Marinade: Process first 9 ingredients in blender until very finely chopped and almost paste-like consistency. Makes 2 cups (500 mL) marinade. Pour into extra-large resealable freezer bag.

Add chops. Seal. Turn until coated. Marinate in refrigerator for at least 4 hours, turning several times. Drain and discard marinade.

Sprinkle both sides of chops with salt. Preheat gas barbecue to medium. Place chops on greased grill. Cook for about 5 minutes per side until desired doneness. Makes about 8 chops. Serves 4 to 6.

1 serving: 415 Calories; 24.9 g Total Fat (13.1 g Mono, 5.3 g Poly, 4.8 g Sat); 119 mg Cholesterol; 6 g Carbohydrate; 1 g Fibre; 40 g Protein; 335 mg Sodium

Grilled Sausages

The savoury glaze that coats these large sausages is a bit spicy with a very subtle sweetness. The dark grill marks on the outside are very attractive.

GLAZE		
Chili sauce	1/3 cup	75 mL
Water	1/3 cup	75 mL
Apple cider vinegar	3 tbsp.	50 mL
Cooking oil	2 tbsp.	30 mL
Worcestershire sauce	1 tbsp.	15 mL
Brown sugar, packed	1 tbsp.	15 mL
Prepared mustard	2 tsp.	10 mL
Paprika	1 tsp.	5 mL
Onion powder	1 tsp.	5 mL
Pepper	1/4 tsp.	1 mL
Large pork breakfast sausages (about 1 1/4 – 1 1/2 lbs., 560 – 680 g)	8	8
Water, to cover		

Glaze: Combine first 10 ingredients in small bowl. Makes about 1 cup (250 mL) glaze.

Pierce each sausage with fork in 3 or 4 places. Put into large saucepan. Add water. Bring to a boil. Boil, uncovered, for 10 minutes. Drain. Preheat electric grill for 5 minutes or gas barbecue to medium-high. Place sausages on greased grill. Cook for about 15 minutes, turning several times and brushing with glaze, until browned and glazed. Makes 8 sausages.

1 sausage: 276 Calories; 26 g Total Fat (12.4 g Mono, 4 g Poly, 8.3 g Sat); 38 mg Cholesterol; 4 g Carbohydrate; trace Fibre; 7 g Protein; 448 mg Sodium

Variation: Place sausages on greased broiler pan. Broil on top rack in oven for about 7 minutes per side, brushing several times with glaze, until browned and glazed.

Paré Pointer
They stole a bunch of sausage and found a missing link.

Cantonese Pork

These delicious glazed and seasoned pork slices have an authentic
Chinese flavour. Serve them hot as a main course or cold with a salad.

Boneless pork loin roast, trimmed of fat	1 1/2 lbs.	680 g
MARINADE		
Hoisin sauce	1/4 cup	60 mL
Brown sugar, packed	1/4 cup	60 mL
Water	2 tbsp.	30 mL
Oyster sauce	2 tbsp.	30 mL
Sake (rice wine) or dry sherry	2 tbsp.	30 mL
Chinese five-spice powder	1/2 tsp.	2 mL

Cut roast almost in half lengthwise, but not quite through, to other side. Press open to flatten. Make shallow diagonal cuts across both sides at 3/4 inch (2 cm) intervals. Repeat in opposite direction to form diamond pattern. Place in large resealable freezer bag.

Marinade: Combine all 6 ingredients in small bowl. Makes 3/4 cup (175 mL) marinade. Pour over roast. Seal. Turn until coated. Marinate in refrigerator overnight, turning several times. Drain marinade into small saucepan. Bring to a boil. Reduce heat to medium-low. Simmer, uncovered, for about 30 minutes until reduced by half and slightly thickened. Preheat gas barbecue to medium. Place roast on greased grill. Close lid. Cook for about 40 minutes, turning several times and brushing with marinade, until meat thermometer inserted in centre reads 155°F (68°C) or until desired doneness. Cover with foil. Let stand for 10 minutes. Internal temperature should rise to at least 160°F (70°C). Slice thinly on diagonal. Makes six 3 oz. (85 g) servings.

1 serving: 312 Calories; 4.4 g Total Fat (1.9 g Mono, 0.6 g Poly, 1.5 g Sat); 79 mg Cholesterol; 16 g Carbohydrate; trace Fibre; 26 g Protein; 295 mg Sodium

 tip
When barbecuing or grilling pork, remember the words low and slow. Grilling over low to medium heat for longer periods of time will produce tender, juicy meat that is evenly cooked. A slower cooking process will protect the meat from unnecessary shrinkage, producing higher cooking yields and providing you with more portions for your money.

Golden Mustard Glazed Ribs

The tiny mustard seed specks that coat these ribs are
visually attractive and they taste very unique. The sweet, sticky
glaze adds to the mild flavour of the meat.

Racks of pork back ribs (about 3 lbs., 1.4 kg), cut into 3 – 6 bone portions	3	3
Water, to cover		
MARINADE		
Fancy (mild) molasses	1/2 cup	125 mL
Grainy mustard	1/2 cup	125 mL
Finely chopped onion	1/3 cup	75 mL
Apple cider vinegar	1/3 cup	75 mL
Worcestershire sauce	2 tbsp.	30 mL
Brown mustard seed	2 tsp.	10 mL

Put ribs into large pot or Dutch oven. Add water. Bring to a boil. Reduce heat. Cover. Simmer for 30 minutes. Drain. Cool slightly. Place in large resealable freezer bags.

Marinade: Combine all 6 ingredients in small bowl. Makes about 2 cups (500 mL) marinade. Pour over ribs. Seal. Turn until coated. Marinate in refrigerator for at least 1 1/2 hours or overnight, turning several times. Drain marinade into small saucepan. Bring to a boil. Reduce heat to medium-low. Simmer, uncovered, for about 15 minutes until reduced and slightly thickened. Preheat gas barbecue to medium-low. Place ribs on greased grill. Close lid. Cook for about 15 minutes, turning several times and brushing with marinade, until glazed. Serves 6.

1 serving: 477 Calories; 18.6 g Total Fat (8.7 g Mono, 2 g Poly, 6.1 g Sat); 111 mg Cholesterol; 23 g Carbohydrate; 1 g Fibre; 53 g Protein; 414 mg Sodium

Variation: Place ribs on greased broiler pan. Broil on second rack in oven for about 15 minutes, turning several times and brushing with marinade, until glazed.

Barbecue Beer Ribs

These sweet, smoky ribs are coated in a crunchy, dark glaze. The addition of beer creates a unique and appealing flavour.

Pork back ribs, cut into 2 – 3 bone portions	4 lbs.	1.8 kg
Water, to cover		
Dry sherry	1 cup	250 mL
MARINADE		
Can of beer	12 1/2 oz.	355 mL
Brown sugar, packed	2/3 cup	150 mL
Soy sauce	1/2 cup	125 mL
Barbecue sauce	1/2 cup	125 mL
Liquid honey	1/4 cup	60 mL
Garlic cloves, minced (or 1/2 – 1 tsp., 2 – 5 mL, powder)	2 – 4	2 – 4

Combine ribs, water and sherry in large pot or Dutch oven. Bring to a boil. Reduce heat to medium-low. Simmer, uncovered, for about 1 1/2 hours, skimming off fat occasionally, until ribs are tender. Remove ribs to wire rack over baking sheet with sides to drain and cool. Discard liquid and solids in pot. Place ribs in large resealable freezer bag.

Marinade: Combine all 6 ingredients in medium saucepan. Heat and stir on medium until boiling and brown sugar is dissolved. Cool. Makes 3 cups (750 mL) marinade. Pour over ribs. Seal. Turn until coated. Marinate in refrigerator for at least 3 hours, turning several times. Remove ribs, reserving 1/2 cup (125 mL) marinade. Preheat gas barbecue to medium-high. Place ribs on greased grill. Close lid. Cook for about 5 minutes per side, brushing with reserved marinade, until heated through. Serves 6.

1 serving: 674 Calories; 23 g Total Fat (10.4 g Mono, 2.5 g Poly, 7.9 g Sat); 143 mg Cholesterol; 43 g Carbohydrate; 1 g Fibre; 67 g Protein; 1490 mg Sodium

Pictured on page 126.

Java Ribs

These unique, saucy ribs are sweet and deliciously sticky.
They are sure to be a hit at your next gathering. Serve with finger
bowls and napkins—you're going to need them!

Pork side spareribs, cut into 3 – 4 bone portions	4 lbs.	1.8 kg
Water, to cover		
Celery rib, chopped	1	1
Small onion, chopped	1	1
Bay leaf	1	1
Dried thyme	1/2 tsp.	2 mL
Salt	1/2 tsp.	2 mL
Pepper	1/2 tsp.	2 mL
JAVA SAUCE		
Prepared triple-strength coffee (see Note)	1 cup	250 mL
Ketchup	3/4 cup	175 mL
Brown sugar, packed	1/2 cup	125 mL
Apple cider vinegar	1/3 cup	75 mL
Hard margarine (or butter)	1/4 cup	60 mL
Worcestershire sauce	2 tbsp.	30 mL
Lemon juice	2 tbsp.	30 mL
Finely grated lemon peel	1 tsp.	5 mL

Combine first 8 ingredients in large pot or Dutch oven. Bring to a boil. Reduce heat. Cover. Simmer for 45 minutes. Drain. Remove and discard bay leaf. Cool.

Java Sauce: Put all 8 ingredients into medium saucepan. Stir. Bring to a boil. Reduce heat. Simmer, uncovered, for 15 minutes, stirring occasionally. Cool. Makes 2 2/3 cups (650 mL) sauce. Pour sauce into large resealable freezer bag. Add spareribs. Seal. Turn until coated. Marinate in refrigerator for at least 3 hours, turning several times. Remove spareribs, reserving sauce. Preheat electric grill for 5 minutes or gas barbecue to medium-high. Place spareribs on greased grill. Cook for about 20 minutes, turning once and brushing several times with sauce, until sizzling and glazed. Discard remaining sauce. Serves 8.

1 serving: 493 Calories; 24.5 g Total Fat (10.1 g Mono, 2.3 g Poly, 10.1 g Sat); 162 mg Cholesterol; 23 g Carbohydrate; 1 g Fibre; 44 g Protein; 649 mg Sodium

Note: If using instant coffee, stir 2 tbsp. (30 mL) granules into 1 cup (250 mL) boiling water for triple strength.

Variation: Spareribs may be marinated at room temperature for 30 minutes.

Fruit-Stuffed Pork Loin

This moist roast contains visible layers of pineapple and apple. The sweet filling is balanced nicely by the smoky barbecue flavour of the roast.

Boneless pork loin roast	4 1/2 lbs.	2 kg
Coarse dry bread crumbs	2 cups	500 mL
Chopped pecans, toasted (see Tip, page 105)	2/3 cup	150 mL
Hard margarine (or butter), melted	1/3 cup	75 mL
Apple juice	1/4 cup	60 mL
Salt	1/4 tsp.	1 mL
Can of pineapple slices, drained	14 oz.	398 mL
Tart medium cooking apples (such as Granny Smith), peeled, cored and thinly sliced	2	2
MARINADE		
Port	1 cup	250 mL
Apple cider	1/2 cup	125 mL
Grainy mustard	1/4 cup	60 mL
Liquid honey	3 tbsp.	50 mL
Cooking oil	2 tbsp.	30 mL
Salt	1 tsp.	5 mL

Cut roast in half lengthwise through centre to form 2 long pieces.

Combine next 5 ingredients in medium bowl. Lay 1 pork piece, cut side up, on work surface. Place 1/2 of bread crumb mixture down centre of cut side.

Layer pineapple and apple slices over bread crumb mixture. Top with remaining bread crumb mixture and remaining pork piece cut side down. Tie with butcher's string at 1 1/4 inch (3 cm) intervals.

Marinade: Combine all 6 ingredients in large shallow dish. Add pork. Turn until coated. Cover. Marinate in refrigerator for at least 6 hours or overnight, turning several times. Drain marinade into medium saucepan. Bring to a boil. Boil for 5 minutes. Preheat gas barbecue to medium-high. Turn off centre or left burner. Place pork, fat-side up, on greased grill over drip pan on unlit side. Close lid. Cook for 30 minutes. Turn pork, brushing liberally with marinade. Cook for about 50 minutes, brushing several times with marinade, until meat thermometer inserted in centre of pork (not stuffing) reads 155°F (68°C) or until desired doneness. Cover with foil. Let stand for 10 minutes. Internal temperature should rise to at least 160°F (70°C). Cut into 1/2 inch (12 mm) thick slices. Serves 8.

1 serving: 735 Calories; 28.4 g Total Fat (12.8 g Mono, 4.6 g Poly, 8.8 g Sat); 196 mg Cholesterol; 49 g Carbohydrate; 3 g Fibre; 61 g Protein; 930 mg Sodium

Barbecue Glazed Ham

This golden, glazed ham will be the centrepiece of your meal. Great for a crowd.

Maple (or maple-flavoured) syrup	1/2 cup	125 mL
Reserved pineapple juice	1/2 cup	125 mL
Dry mustard	1 tbsp.	15 mL
Balsamic vinegar	1 tbsp.	15 mL
Cooked leg of ham, rind removed	10 lbs.	4.5 kg
Can of sliced pineapple, drained and juice reserved, slices cut into 8 pieces each	14 oz.	398 mL
Whole cloves, approximately	3 tbsp.	50 mL

Combine first 4 ingredients in small bowl. Set aside.

Make shallow diagonal cuts across ham at 3/4 inch (2 cm) intervals. Repeat in opposite direction to form diamond pattern.

Place 1 pineapple piece where diagonal cuts meet. Push 1 clove through pineapple to secure. Place ham on wire rack in foil roasting pan. Brush with maple syrup mixture. Preheat gas barbecue to medium. Turn off centre or left burner. Place ham with pan on ungreased grill on unlit side. Close lid. Cook for 45 minutes. Brush with maple syrup mixture. Cook for about 30 minutes, brushing several times with maple syrup mixture, until meat thermometer inserted in centre reads 140°F (60°C) and ham is glazed and golden brown. Cover with foil. Let stand for 10 minutes. Internal temperature should rise to 150°F (65°C). Serves 14 to 16.

1 serving: 468 Calories; 18.1 g Total Fat (8.5 g Mono, 1.8 g Poly, 5.8 g Sat); 170 mg Cholesterol; 20 g Carbohydrate; 1 g Fibre; 54 g Protein; 3592 mg Sodium

Pictured on page 90.

Paré Pointer
Our flowers are as lazy as yours. They are always in beds.

Pepper Pork Skewers

These moist, colourful skewers are perfectly grilled and very tangy.
Serve with Nutty Rice Pilaf, page 140.

Boneless shoulder butt roast, trimmed of fat and cut into 1 inch (2.5 cm) cubes	1 1/2 lbs.	680 g
Peppers (your choice), cut into 1 – 1 1/2 inch (2.5 – 3.8 cm) squares	3	3
Bamboo skewers (8 inch, 20 cm, length), soaked in water for 10 minutes	6	6
BASTING SAUCE		
Lemon juice	1/4 cup	60 mL
Cooking oil	1 tbsp.	15 mL
Garlic cloves, minced (or 3/4 tsp., 4 mL, powder)	3	3
Lemon pepper	2 tsp.	10 mL
Dried whole oregano	1 tsp.	5 mL
Salt	1/2 tsp.	2 mL
Finely grated lemon zest	1/2 tsp.	2 mL

Thread pork cubes and pepper squares alternately onto skewers.

Basting Sauce: Combine all 7 ingredients in small bowl. Makes about 1/3 cup (75 mL) sauce. Preheat gas barbecue to medium-low. Place skewers on greased grill. Close lid. Cook for about 30 minutes, turning every 5 minutes and brushing with sauce, until pork is tender and edges of peppers are slightly charred. Serves 6.

1 serving: 220 Calories; 10 g Total Fat (4.7 g Mono, 1.6 g Poly, 2.8 g Sat); 71 mg Cholesterol; 7 g Carbohydrate; 1 g Fibre; 25 g Protein; 239 mg Sodium

Pictured on page 126.

 When barbecuing or grilling kabobs, make sure to leave a small space between the food threaded onto the skewers. This will allow the heat to circulate around the food, cooking all pieces evenly.

Pork Satay

These kabobs are brushed with a thick, peanut-flavoured satay sauce.
Serve with lime wedges to add some colour to this dish.

Pork tenderloin, cut into 3/4 inch (2 cm) cubes	2 lbs.	900 g
Bamboo skewers (8 inch, 20 cm, length), soaked in water for 10 minutes	10	10
SATAY SAUCE		
Peanut (or cooking) oil	1 tbsp.	15 mL
Stalk of lemon grass, bulb only (root and stalk removed), bruised and finely chopped (or 1 tsp., 5 mL, finely grated lemon peel)	1	1
Ground cumin	1 tsp.	5 mL
Prepared chicken broth	1 1/3 cups	325 mL
Crunchy peanut butter (see Note)	1/2 cup	125 mL
Sweet (or regular) chili sauce	3 tbsp.	50 mL
Lime juice	1 tbsp.	15 mL

Thread pork onto skewers.

Satay Sauce: Heat peanut oil in medium saucepan on medium. Add lemon grass and cumin. Heat and stir for 2 to 3 minutes until fragrant.

Add broth, peanut butter and chili sauce. Stir. Simmer, uncovered, for 3 to 5 minutes until thickened. Remove from heat.

Add lime juice. Stir. Makes about 2 cups (500 mL) sauce. Brush each kabob with sauce. Preheat electric grill for 5 minutes or gas barbecue to medium. Place kabobs on greased grill. Cook for about 15 minutes, turning often, until desired doneness. Makes 10 kabobs.

1 kabob: 213 Calories; 10.7 g Total Fat (4.9 g Mono, 2.7 g Poly, 2.4 g Sat); 53 mg Cholesterol; 4 g Carbohydrate; 1 g Fibre; 26 g Protein; 220 mg Sodium

Note: Add finely chopped peanuts to smooth peanut butter if you don't have crunchy on hand.

Garlic Pork Kabob Pitas

Place the kabobs, warmed pita breads, sauce and vegetables
on the table and let guests build their own pita wraps.
This recipe is well worth the effort. Fun party food.

MARINADE

Plain yogurt	2/3 cup	150 mL
Lemon juice	1/4 cup	60 mL
Olive (or cooking) oil	3 tbsp.	50 mL
Chopped fresh thyme leaves (or 3/4 – 1 1/2 tsp., 4 – 7 mL, dried)	1 – 2 tbsp.	15 – 30 mL
Garlic cloves, minced (or 1/2 – 1 tsp., 2 – 5 mL, powder)	2 – 4	2 – 4
Chili paste (sambal oelek)	1/2 tsp.	2 mL
Salt	1/4 tsp.	1 mL
Pork leg, trimmed of fat and cut into 3/4 inch (2 cm) cubes	1 1/2 lbs.	680 g
Bamboo skewers (8 inch, 20 cm, length), soaked in water for 10 minutes	8	8

TOMATO SAUCE

Medium roma (plum) tomatoes, halved lengthwise	6	6
Fresh green chilies, halved and seeds removed (see Note)	2	2
Garlic clove, minced (or 1/4 tsp., 1 mL, powder)	1	1
Plain yogurt	1/2 cup	125 mL
Finely chopped fresh parsley (or 2 1/4 tsp., 11 mL, flakes)	3 tbsp.	50 mL
Lemon juice	2 tbsp.	30 mL
Granulated sugar	1 tsp.	5 mL
Salt	1/4 tsp.	1 mL
Pepper	1/4 tsp.	1 mL
Pita breads, warmed	8	8
English cucumber (with peel), thinly sliced	1/2	1/2
Medium tomatoes, sliced	3	3

(continued on next page)

138 On The Grill

Marinade: Combine first 7 ingredients in large shallow dish. Makes 1 1/3 cups (325 mL) marinade.

Thread pork onto skewers. Add to marinade. Turn until coated. Cover. Marinate in refrigerator for at least 6 hours or overnight, turning several times. Drain and discard marinade.

Tomato Sauce: Place tomato halves, cut side up, and green chili halves on ungreased baking sheet. Spray with cooking spray. Bake in 400°F (205°C) oven for about 30 minutes until softened. Cool slightly. Transfer to blender.

Add next 7 ingredients. Process until smooth. Makes 2 cups (500 mL) sauce. Preheat electric grill for 5 minutes or gas barbecue to medium-high. Place kabobs on greased grill. Cook for 10 to 15 minutes, turning occasionally, until pork is tender.

Spread top of each pita with 1/4 cup (60 mL) sauce. Divide and layer cucumber and tomato slices on top of sauce. Remove pork from skewers and place on top of tomato. Makes 8 pitas.

1 pita: 365 Calories; 10 g Total Fat (5.7 g Mono, 1.2 g Poly, 2.2 g Sat); 70 mg Cholesterol; 42 g Carbohydrate; 2 g Fibre; 27 g Protein; 518 mg Sodium

Note: Wear gloves when chopping green chilies and avoid touching your eyes.

 tip

To reduce the fat content of your meals, try grilling, stir-frying, roasting, braising or broiling your pork. These cooking methods either allow the fat to drip away or require little added fats or oils during the cooking process. Also, trim the visible fat from your pork before cooking and use a non-stick wok or frying pan when frying or stir-frying. This way, little or no added oil will be needed to keep your ingredients from sticking to the pan.

Nutty Rice Pilaf

This is a well-seasoned blend of rice, vegetables and toasted almonds.
This light, fluffy dish would go so well with Pepper Pork Skewers, page 136.

Cooking oil	2 tsp.	10 mL
Sesame oil	2 tsp.	10 mL
Diced onion	1/4 cup	60 mL
Diced carrot	1/4 cup	60 mL
Hard margarine (or butter)	2 tbsp.	30 mL
Long grain brown rice	2 cups	500 mL
Salt	1/2 tsp.	2 mL
Ground cumin	1/4 tsp.	1 mL
Ground coriander	1/4 tsp.	1 mL
Prepared chicken (or vegetable) broth	4 cups	1 L
Chopped fresh parsley (or 3/4 tsp., 4 mL, flakes)	1 tbsp.	15 mL
Slivered almonds, toasted (see Tip, page 105)	1/4 cup	60 mL

Heat cooking oil and sesame oil in large frying pan on medium. Add onion and carrot. Cook for about 2 minutes until onion is softened. Transfer to greased 2 quart (2 L) casserole.

Melt margarine in same frying pan. Add rice. Cook for about 4 minutes, stirring frequently, until colour deepens. Add salt, cumin and coriander. Heat and stir until rice is toasted. Add to onion mixture. Stir.

Add broth. Cover. Bake in 350°F (175°C) oven for about 1 1/2 hours until rice is tender and broth is absorbed. Fluff with fork.

Sprinkle with parsley and almonds. Makes 8 cups (2 L).

1/2 cup (125 mL): 135 Calories; 4.8 g Total Fat (2.1 g Mono, 1 g Poly, 1.4 g Sat); 4 mg Cholesterol; 19 g Carbohydrate; 1 g Fibre; 4 g Protein; 282 mg Sodium

Pictured on page 126.

Peach Chutney

This fresh, tangy chutney is sweet and sour with a slight hint of spice. It is the perfect accompaniment to roasted pork.

Fresh peaches (about 2 lbs., 900 g)	8	8
Boiling water		
Ice water		
Medium onions, chopped	2	2
Brown sugar, packed	1 1/4 cups	300 mL
White vinegar	1/2 cup	125 mL
Curry powder	2 tbsp.	30 mL
Garam masala	1 1/2 tsp.	7 mL
Lemon juice	1/4 cup	60 mL
Finely grated lemon zest	2 tsp.	10 mL
Salt	1 1/2 tsp.	7 mL

Blanch peaches in boiling water in large pot or Dutch oven for about 30 to 60 seconds until skins start to loosen. Drain.

Hold under cold water and peel or plunge into ice water in large bowl. Let stand for 10 minutes until cold. Drain. Peel and discard skins. Chop peaches. Put into same pot.

Add next 5 ingredients. Stir. Bring to a boil. Boil, uncovered, for 20 to 25 minutes, stirring occasionally, until thickened.

Add lemon juice, lemon zest and salt. Stir. Fill hot sterilized jars to within 1/2 inch (12 mm) of top. Place sterilized metal lids on jars and screw metal bands on securely. Process in boiling water bath for 10 minutes. Makes 6 half pint (1 cup, 250 mL) jars.

2 tbsp. (30 mL): 31 Calories; 0.1 g Total Fat (0 g Mono, 0 g Poly, 0 g Sat); 0 mg Cholesterol; 8 g Carbohydrate; trace Fibre; trace Protein; 69 mg Sodium

Paré Pointer

Susie didn't want to go to school. She was afraid of the school spirit.

Mushroom Tarragon Sauce

*This rich, full-flavoured sauce goes well
with grilled pork chops or tenderloin.*

Olive (or cooking) oil	1 tbsp.	15 mL
Hard margarine (or butter)	1 tbsp.	15 mL
Brown (or white) mushrooms, sliced	2 cups	500 mL
Dry white (or alcohol-free) wine	1/2 cup	125 mL
Whipping cream	1 1/4 cups	300 mL
Chopped fresh tarragon leaves (or	2 – 3 tsp.	10 – 15 mL
1/2 – 3/4 tsp., 2 – 4 mL, dried)		
Salt	1/4 tsp.	1 mL
Pepper	1/8 tsp.	0.5 mL

Heat olive oil and margarine in large frying pan on medium. Add
mushrooms. Cook for 5 to 10 minutes, stirring occasionally, until browned.

Add wine. Stir. Heat for about 5 minutes until wine is mostly evaporated.

Add remaining 4 ingredients. Heat and stir for 5 to 7 minutes until boiling
and thickened. Makes about 1 cup (250 mL).

*2 tbsp. (30 mL): 158 Calories; 15.4 g Total Fat (5.2 g Mono, 0.6 g Poly, 8.7 g Sat); 48 mg Cholesterol;
2 g Carbohydrate; trace Fibre; 1 g Protein; 89 mg Sodium*

Pictured on page 107.

1. Spinach And Pear Salad, page 47
2. Mediterranean Pie, page 97

Props Courtesy Of: Casa Bugatti

Tomato Pear Relish

This dark golden relish has a wonderful combination of flavours and textures.
Use it to spruce up a roast pork sandwich or spread it over plain ham slices.

Firm medium pears, peeled and chopped	4	4
Medium tomatoes, chopped	4	4
Medium onions, chopped	2	2
Brown sugar, packed	2 cups	500 mL
Raisins, chopped	1 cup	250 mL
White vinegar	1 cup	250 mL
Brown mustard seed	3 tbsp.	50 mL
Ground coriander	1 tsp.	5 mL
Ground ginger	1 tsp.	5 mL
Salt	1 tsp.	5 mL
Ground cinnamon	1/2 tsp.	2 mL

Combine all 11 ingredients in large pot or Dutch oven. Heat and stir on medium for about 5 minutes until brown sugar is dissolved. Bring to a boil. Boil, uncovered, for about 50 minutes, stirring occasionally, until thickened. Fill hot sterilized jars to within 1/2 inch (12 mm) of top. Place sterilized metal lids on jars and screw metal bands on securely. Process in boiling water bath for 10 minutes. Makes 6 half pint (1 cup, 250 mL) jars.

2 tbsp. (30 mL): 61 Calories; 0.3 g Total Fat (0.2 g Mono, 0.1 g Poly, 0 g Sat); 0 mg Cholesterol; 15 g Carbohydrate; 1 g Fibre; 1 g Protein; 52 mg Sodium

Pictured on page 90.

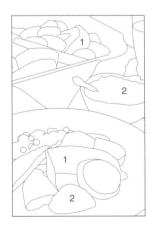

1. Roasted Pork Chops, page 74
2. Chunky Applesauce, page 148

Props Courtesy Of: Pyrex ® Bakeware

Green Tomato Pickle

This delicious, chunky relish is sweet, spicy,
salty and sour—all at the same time!

Boiling water	7 cups	1.75 L
Coarse (pickling) salt	1/2 cup	125 mL
Green tomatoes, peeled and chopped	8	8
Large onions, chopped	2	2
Brown sugar, packed	2 cups	500 mL
White vinegar	2 cups	500 mL
Finely grated peeled gingerroot	2 tsp.	10 mL
All-purpose flour	1/3 cup	75 mL
Curry powder	2 tsp.	10 mL
Turmeric	1 tsp.	5 mL
Ground allspice	1/2 tsp.	2 mL
Cayenne pepper	1/4 – 1/2 tsp.	1 – 2 mL
White vinegar	1/3 cup	75 mL

Combine boiling water and salt in large bowl. Add tomato and onion. Stir. Cover. Chill overnight. Drain.

Combine brown sugar, first amount of vinegar and ginger in large pot or Dutch oven. Heat and stir on medium until brown sugar is dissolved. Add tomato mixture. Stir. Bring to a boil.

Measure remaining 6 ingredients into small bowl. Stir until consistency of smooth paste. Add to tomato mixture. Stir until boiling and slightly thickened. Boil, uncovered, for about 25 minutes until thickened. Fill hot sterilized jars to within 1/2 inch (12 mm) of top. Place sterilized metal lids on jars and screw metal bands on securely. Process in boiling water bath for 10 minutes. Makes 10 half pint (1 cup, 250 mL) jars.

2 tbsp. (30 mL): 28 Calories; 0 g Total Fat (0 g Mono, 0 g Poly, 0 g Sat); 0 mg Cholesterol; 7 g Carbohydrate; trace Fibre; trace Protein; 714 mg Sodium

Pictured on page 54.

Creamy Applesauce

This velvety smooth sauce has a wonderful, tart apple flavour.

Sweet apple cider	1 cup	250 mL
Tart medium cooking apples (such as Granny Smith), peeled, cored and sliced	4	4
Dry white (or alcohol-free) wine	1/2 cup	125 mL
Prepared chicken broth	1/2 cup	125 mL
Brandy (or 1 tsp., 5 mL, flavouring)	1/4 cup	60 mL
Hard margarine (or butter)	2 tbsp.	30 mL
Whipping cream	1/2 cup	125 mL
Salt	1/2 tsp.	2 mL
Pepper, dash		

Measure cider into large saucepan. Bring to a boil. Boil, uncovered, on medium for about 10 minutes until reduced to 1/3 cup (75 mL).

Add next 4 ingredients. Cook, uncovered, for about 10 minutes, stirring occasionally, until apple is very soft. Cool slightly. Process in blender until smooth. Return to saucepan.

Add remaining 4 ingredients. Heat and stir on medium for 5 to 10 minutes until hot and beginning to boil. Makes about 3 cups (750 mL).

2 tbsp. (30 mL): 54 Calories; 2.6 g Total Fat (1.1 g Mono, 0.2 g Poly, 1.2 g Sat); 6 mg Cholesterol; 6 g Carbohydrate; trace Fibre; trace Protein; 67 mg Sodium

Pictured on page 125.

Paré Pointer

They teach history by asking you questions about things that happened before you were born.

Chunky Applesauce

This sweet, golden applesauce has a wonderful texture.
The ever-so-subtle hint of brandy adds a special touch to this recipe.

Tart medium cooking apples (such as Granny Smith), peeled, cored and sliced	4	4
Granulated sugar	1/3 cup	75 mL
Water	1/3 cup	75 mL
Brandy (or 1/2 tsp., 2 mL, flavouring)	2 tbsp.	30 mL
Salt	1/2 tsp.	2 mL

Combine all 5 ingredients in large saucepan. Heat and stir on medium until sugar is dissolved. Cook, uncovered, for about 15 minutes until thickened and apple is very soft. Makes about 1 1/3 cups (325 mL).

2 tbsp. (30 mL): 54 Calories; 0.1 g Total Fat (0 g Mono, 0 g Poly, 0 g Sat); 0 mg Cholesterol; 13 g Carbohydrate; 1 g Fibre; trace Protein; 86 mg Sodium

Pictured on page 144.

Apricot Sauce

This tangy, versatile sauce has a distinct vinegar
flavour that would go very well with a baked ham or roast pork.

Apricot jam	1 cup	250 mL
Apple cider vinegar	3 tbsp.	50 mL
Paprika	1/4 tsp.	1 mL

Combine jam, vinegar and paprika in small bowl. Rub through sieve to make smooth. Makes about 1 cup (250 mL).

2 tbsp. (30 mL): 103 Calories; 0.1 g Total Fat (0 g Mono, 0 g Poly, 0 g Sat); 0 mg Cholesterol; 28 g Carbohydrate; 0 g Fibre; trace Protein; 17 mg Sodium

Pictured on page 89.

PLUM SAUCE: Use same amount of plum jam instead of apricot jam. Omit paprika. Particularly good when served with Spicy Sausage Rolls, page 14, or Sweet Cold Pork Slices, page 15.

Cranberry Ham Glaze

Use half of this deep red, sweet sauce to baste a large piece of ham or individual ham slices. Serve the other half in a bowl on the table. Your guests will love its smooth, thick consistency and its warm, inviting flavour.

Can of whole cranberry sauce	14 oz.	398 mL
Brown sugar, packed	1 cup	250 mL
Dry red (or alcohol-free) wine	1/2 cup	125 mL
Prepared mustard	2 tsp.	10 mL

Combine all 4 ingredients in small saucepan. Bring to a boil, stirring often. Reduce heat to medium-low. Simmer, uncovered, for 5 minutes, stirring occasionally. Makes 2 2/3 cups (650 mL).

2 tbsp. (30 mL): 76 Calories; 0 g Total Fat (0 g Mono, 0 g Poly, 0 g Sat); 0 mg Cholesterol; 19 g Carbohydrate; trace Fibre; trace Protein; 16 mg Sodium

Tutti-Frutti Ham Glaze

This sweet, thick glaze has a delicious peach flavour. Brush it on ham steaks while they're grilling or baking for a scrumptious meal.

Brown sugar, packed	1/2 cup	125 mL
All-purpose flour	2 tbsp.	30 mL
Frozen concentrated orange juice, thawed	1/4 cup	60 mL
Peach jam	1 cup	250 mL

Combine brown sugar and flour in small saucepan. Stir in orange juice concentrate and jam. Heat and stir on medium for about 5 minutes until boiling and thickened. Cool. Process in blender until smooth if desired. Makes 1 2/3 cups (400 mL).

2 tbsp. (30 mL): 119 Calories; 0 g Total Fat (0 g Mono, 0 g Poly, 0 g Sat); 0 mg Cholesterol; 30 g Carbohydrate; trace Fibre; trace Protein; 12 mg Sodium

Measurement Tables

Throughout this book measurements are given in Conventional and Metric measure. To compensate for differences between the two measurements due to rounding, a full metric measure is not always used. The cup used is the standard 8 fluid ounce. Temperature is given in degrees Fahrenheit and Celsius. Baking pan measurements are in inches and centimetres as well as quarts and litres. An exact metric conversion is given below as well as the working equivalent (Metric Standard Measure).

Spoons

Conventional Measure	Metric Exact Conversion Millilitre (mL)	Metric Standard Measure Millilitre (mL)
1/8 teaspoon (tsp.)	0.6 mL	0.5 mL
1/4 teaspoon (tsp.)	1.2 mL	1 mL
1/2 teaspoon (tsp.)	2.4 mL	2 mL
1 teaspoon (tsp.)	4.7 mL	5 mL
2 teaspoons (tsp.)	9.4 mL	10 mL
1 tablespoon (tbsp.)	14.2 mL	15 mL

Cups

Conventional Measure	Metric Exact Conversion Millilitre (mL)	Metric Standard Measure Millilitre (mL)
1/4 cup (4 tbsp.)	56.8 mL	60 mL
1/3 cup (5 1/3 tbsp.)	75.6 mL	75 mL
1/2 cup (8 tbsp.)	113.7 mL	125 mL
2/3 cup (10 2/3 tbsp.)	151.2 mL	150 mL
3/4 cup (12 tbsp.)	170.5 mL	175 mL
1 cup (16 tbsp.)	227.3 mL	250 mL
4 1/2 cups	1022.9 mL	1000 mL (1 L)

Oven Temperatures

Fahrenheit (°F)	Celsius (°C)
175°	80°
200°	95°
225°	110°
250°	120°
275°	140°
300°	150°
325°	160°
350°	175°
375°	190°
400°	205°
425°	220°
450°	230°
475°	240°
500°	260°

Dry Measurements

Conventional Measure Ounces (oz.)	Metric Exact Conversion Grams (g)	Metric Standard Measure Grams (g)
1 oz.	28.3 g	28 g
2 oz.	56.7 g	57 g
3 oz.	85.0 g	85 g
4 oz.	113.4 g	125 g
5 oz.	141.7 g	140 g
6 oz.	170.1 g	170 g
7 oz.	198.4 g	200 g
8 oz.	226.8 g	250 g
16 oz.	453.6 g	500 g
32 oz.	907.2 g	1000 g (1 kg)

Pans

Conventional Inches	Metric Centimetres
8x8 inch	20x20 cm
9x9 inch	22x22 cm
9x13 inch	22x33 cm
10x15 inch	25x38 cm
11x17 inch	28x43 cm
8x2 inch round	20x5 cm
9x2 inch round	22x5 cm
10x4 1/2 inch tube	25x11 cm
8x4x3 inch loaf	20x10x7.5 cm
9x5x3 inch loaf	22x12.5x7.5 cm

Casseroles

CANADA & BRITAIN		UNITED STATES	
Standard Size Casserole	Exact Metric Measure	Standard Size Casserole	Exact Metric Measure
1 qt. (5 cups)	1.13 L	1 qt. (4 cups)	900 mL
1 1/2 qts. (7 1/2 cups)	1.69 L	1 1/2 qts. (6 cups)	1.35 L
2 qts. (10 cups)	2.25 L	2 qts. (8 cups)	1.8 L
2 1/2 qts. (12 1/2 cups)	2.81 L	2 1/2 qts. (10 cups)	2.25 L
3 qts. (15 cups)	3.38 L	3 qts. (12 cups)	2.7 L
4 qts. (20 cups)	4.5 L	4 qts. (16 cups)	3.6 L
5 qts. (25 cups)	5.63 L	5 qts. (20 cups)	4.5 L

Tip Index

Recipe Index

152

153

155